# SARA BUENFELD'S
# HOME FROM WORK SUPPERS

SARA BUENFELD'S

# HOME FROM WORK SUPPERS

*For Mum, Dad and Graham*

Published in 1995 by Merehurst Limited
Ferry House, 51-57 Lacy Road, Putney, London SW15 1PR



ISBN 1-85391-436-3



A catalogue record for this book is available from the British Library.

Editor: Beverly Le Blanc
Series Designer: Hammond Hammond
Photographer: Graham Kirk
Food prepared for photography by: Sara Buenfeld
Assisted by: Iris Harvey
Stylist: Helen Payne
Typesetter: Michael Weintroub

Colour separation by Global Colour, Malaysia
Printed in Singapore by CS Graphics Pte Ltd

## NOTES

A standard spoon measurement is used in all recipes:

1 teaspoon = one 5 ml spoon
1 tablespoon = one 15 ml spoon
All spoon measures are level.

All eggs are size 3 unless otherwise specified.

Ovens should be preheated to the specified temperature.

For all recipes, quantities are given in metric and Imperial; follow one set of measures but not a mixture as they are not interchangeable.

*Frontispiece: Crab Cakes with Guacamole, see page 57, and Pan-cooked Prawns with Ginger and Coriander, see page 61*

# FOREWORD

Most evenings I come home from work tired, hungry and looking forward to sitting down with a glass of wine and a quickly prepared supper. This is a book dedicated to everyone who feels the same. For everyone who enjoys good food and trying something new; everyone who doesn't want to rely on the pre-packed suppers from supermarkets, but does want to eat within about half an hour of getting home. And, unless you have a microwave, most chilled and frozen suppers take that long to reheat anyway.

Sometimes I fancy a particular kind of cuisine, be it satisfying strands of pasta, something spicy like Mexican, Indian or Thai, or fairly plain dishes to serve with vegetables, so I've brought together a wide collection of my favourite recipes which envelop the tastes and ingredients I like most. And, you'll find all the ingredients used are widely available from large supermarkets. Supermarkets have come a long way since I first started writing about food more than fifteen years ago. Then, if I wanted to cook with any herbs other than parsley I had to grow them myself and garlic was considered 'unusual'. Now practically every time I go shopping I discover something new, so you shouldn't need to make an extra trip to a specialist shop if a recipe calls for fresh ginger or basil, lemon grass or oyster sauce.

The recipes are also designed to serve two. Not just because most of my mid-week meals are shared with my husband, Graham, but because practically everyone I know from my family, to friends and colleagues cook for couples – yet, there are surprisingly few books available that cater for this. That said, however, all the recipes can easily be increased to serve larger numbers.

Although this book is intended to provide you with the recipes for fast suppers, you shouldn't feel that you are in a race against time. It doesn't matter at all if the recipes take a little longer than I suggested because you don't chop as fast as I do, or it takes you a few minutes to find the olive oil. Also, fairly specific timings are included with each recipe to give you an indication of when each stage of the recipe is ready, but cookers vary, so keep a close eye on all the ingredients and judge for yourself when the onions are golden enough, meat and fish are cooked through and the vegetables are just tender. I always gather all the ingredients for a dish together before I start cooking so I can be certain I haven't run out of anything crucial.

Here are a few other points worth bearing in mind to help the preparations run smoothly:

Preheat the oven as soon as possible so it is at the correct temperature when you are ready to start cooking.

When you have a time gap while something is cooking, toss together a quick salad or put the vegetables in a steamer.

Finally, once the meal is ready, it doesn't take more than a few minutes to light candles to create a cosy atmosphere in the winter (even if one eye is on the telly), or set the table in the garden to enjoy the last of the evening sunshine – you'll appreciate your speedy supper all the more.

Sara Buenfeld

# Fish and shellfish

# Risottos, pizzas and pastas

# Vegetarian main dishes



# Index

# INTRODUCTION

Food has been a passion of mine for as long as I can remember. It's my job – I'm the Food and Drink Editor of *Living* magazine – it's my hobby and it's a constant source of inspiration every time I eat out or discover a new ingredient. But that doesn't mean I want to be in the kitchen to the exclusion of everything else, especially when I'm tired after a day in the office or the photographic studio preparing food for the pictures in the magazine. What I need then are dishes that are quick to make, tasty and don't require a lot of shopping. All of the recipes in this book are just that – designed to be on the table within about 30 minutes or less from the time you start cooking.

Some of these recipes have been favourites of mine for years, while others are based on meals I've enjoyed in restaurants, on holiday or with friends. I've also written some specifically for this book. This is a collection of some very basic recipes and others that are a bit more special. However, they're all easy and achievable, even if you are not very experienced in the kitchen. And, you don't need a cupboard of special equipment, but I do think a non-stick frying pan is essential.

Although I own a microwave, I don't actually use it very often. This is mainly because I enjoy the enticing aromas and all the stirring, simmering and sizzling that goes on during conventional cooking. But I couldn't do without it for quickly defrosting meat, fish and poultry, as I often decide on impulse what to cook for supper when I look in the fridge, freezer and store cupboard when I get home from work.

## SHOPPING AND FRESH INGREDIENTS

The first stage of fast cooking is choosing the appropriate ingredients. Quick-cooking prime cuts of meat like lean lamb and pork steaks and boneless chicken breasts are perfect for grilling, pan-frying and stir-frying, but unfortunately they do cost more than the slower-cooking, tougher cuts or portions with bones. For speed and convenience, however, you can't beat them: there's no wastage, and they are relatively no more expensive than using prepared meals from the supermarket.

When I'm doing my weekly shop, I always rummage at the back of the chill cabinet for the items with the longest sell-by dates so they will last for at least a couple of days after I get them home, and then I use up the most perishable ingredients as the week progresses. Towards the end of the week, I cook bacon, cheese or store cupboard dishes, or rely on my freezer for meat, fish or poultry, and meals like chilli that I have made and frozen.

I'm very fortunate as I pass an excellent supermarket on my way home from work each day, so I can pop in, pick up fresh ingredients like fish (I ask the assistant at the fish counter to bone and skin it for me to save time in the kitchen), or grab some crusty bread. I also try to keep a supply of partially-baked breads in the freezer, such as Italian ciabatta, an olive oil bread, or French sticks, because they are baked within minutes to serve with suppers like salads, pasta dishes and risottos.

Fresh vegetables and fruit are the next part of my weekly shop, as I look for ingredients not just to use in recipes but also for serving as salads and accompaniments. I have a very simple steamer that expands to fit inside my saucepans, and I often steam a selection of vegetables together in one pan because with this quick-cooking technique there isn't any transfer of flavours, the vegetables taste a hundred times better than boiled, and it saves on washing up!

If you are planning to serve rice or potatoes or steam vegetables, put a saucepan of water over high heat, covered, to bring to the boil as soon as possible. It's easy to under-estimate how long this can take.

Fresh herbs also play an important role in my style of cooking. I grow hardy herbs like sage, rosemary, thyme and bay in tubs outside the back door, and the soft-leaf varieties like basil, parsley and mint in the garden during the summer months and unpredictably on my kitchen windowsill in the winter, when I top up my supply at the supermarket with small packets. For fresh coriander, however, I'm rather more ambitious and buy large bunches, mainly because of my love affair with Indian, Thai and Mexican dishes, which require generous quantities. I also keep a supply of ginger and fresh red and green chillies in the crisper in the bottom of the fridge.

### STORE CUPBOARD INGREDIENTS

It's difficult to guess what people classify as store cupboard ingredients, especially after opening a friend's cupboard and finding just a cruet, a bottle of ketchup and a packet of custard powder!

I'm lucky to have an old-fashioned larder and rely on it heavily for my everyday meals, keeping it stocked with several varieties of rice, such as fragrant Indian basmati, American long grain and Italian arborio, as well as bulgar wheat, pasta and Chinese noodles. They're great for basing a meal on as well as serving as accompaniments.

I also have quite a few oils open at any one time, such as olive and sunflower oils for cooking, extra-virgin olive oils and nut oils for salad dressings and sesame oil for using in Oriental dishes.

I rarely have the time or bones to make stock, so I tend to use fresh stocks that are sold in cartons at the supermarket, or make it from good-quality cubes that are light in flavour and colour and free from artifical ingredients like monosodium glutamate.

I don't tend to use a lot of canned foods, except for tuna, tomatoes, beans and occasionally sweetcorn. However, I couldn't do without my spices, particularly coriander and cumin, which I've been known to take camping and on sailing holidays!

Then, of course, there are other enticing flavourings, such as soy and fish sauces, sun-dried tomatoes, peanut butter and creamed coconut, which I always like to have to hand. You'll find explanations and descriptions at the bottom of appropriate recipes if I have used anything you might not be familiar with. My general advice is to make the most of whatever storage space you have. If you have a well-stocked store cupboard, you always have the start of a delicious meal. It also means less shopping and you will have the ingredients to inspire your creativity when you are in the mood for improvising.

# Chicken, turkey and duck

From spicy curries to fast stir-fries and simple yet tasty dishes to serve with vegetables, chicken is an important ingredient in my everyday cooking. It's healthy, economical and cooks quickly. Turkey and boneless duck breasts are also favourite ingredients, so I've included recipes for them, too.

# THAI CHICKEN WITH BASIL AND CHILLIES

Time to make: 20 minutes
Time to cook: about 10 minutes

Serves 2

**2 boneless, skinless chicken breasts**

**2 garlic cloves**

**1 to 2 fresh green chillies**

**1 large red pepper**

**90 g (3 oz) small sugar snap peas or mange-touts**

**4 spring onions**

**7 g (¼ oz) fresh basil**

**1 teaspoon cornflour**

**2 tablespoons fish sauce or light soy sauce**

**1 tablespoon sesame oil**

**1 teaspoon ground coriander**

**1 tablespoon soft brown sugar**

*Thai Chicken with Basil and Chillies ready for serving.*

A year or so ago, it was almost impossible to re-create Thai dishes at home without first making a special trip to an Oriental food shop to buy the correct ingredients. Now, thankfully, fresh lemon grass, fish sauce, fresh chillies and herbs like coriander and basil are widely available from large supermarkets, making shopping a whole lot easier. I like to serve this fragrant stir-fry with boiled or stir-fried rice or egg noodles tossed with a little sesame oil.

**1** First prepare the ingredients because once you start cooking everything will happen very quickly. Slice the chicken into bite-size strips. Shred the garlic, seed and finely chop the chillies and core, seed and roughly chop the red pepper. Top and tail the sugar snap peas or mange-touts. Chop the spring onions at a slight angle to make fine shreds, then shred the basil.
**2** Mix the cornflour with the fish or soy sauce until smooth.
**3** Heat the oil in a wok or large saucepan over a high heat until very hot, then toss in the chicken, garlic and chillies and stir-fry for 2 minutes until the chicken changes colour.
**4** Add the red pepper, sugar snap peas or mange-touts, spring onions, ground coriander and sugar and stir-fry for 4 to 5 minutes longer. Stir the cornflour mixture, then pour it into the chicken and vegetables, stirring constantly until the juices thicken.
**5** Toss in the basil, remove from the heat and serve immediately.

### Cook's Tip

Fish sauce, a salty, distinctively flavoured thin brown liquid made from salted fish or shrimps, is used in Thailand in much the same way that soy sauce is used in China. It is pungent, and to be honest, quite off-putting sniffed straight from the bottle, but delicious and well worth buying for adding an authentic flavour to Thai and Vietnamese recipes, such as curries, soups and stir-fries. The bottles from Thai stores are quite large, so it's worth looking out for smaller bottles in the Oriental section of large supermarkets unless you have a lot of storage space or intend to do lots of Thai cooking.

# CURRIED CHICKEN MAYONNAISE WITH PEACHES

Time to make: 20 minutes
No cooking

Serves 2

**¼ cucumber**

**salt**

**125 g (4 oz) Greek-style yogurt**

**3 tablespoons mayonnaise**

**3 teaspoons mild curry paste**

**1 tablespoon peach or mango chutney**

**1 piece stem ginger**

**250 g (8 oz) cooked chicken or turkey, preferably breast meat, skinned**

**1 fresh peach or nectarine**

**30 g (1 oz) salted roasted cashew nuts**

**2 tablespoons chopped fresh coriander**

**salt and freshly ground black pepper**

Food eaten outdoors always tastes that extra bit special, and I often take this as part of a picnic to the open-air classical concerts held in the summer at Crystal Palace, in London. It also makes a refreshing way to use up turkey leftovers at Christmas, but as fresh peaches are not in season then I substitute a fresh mango or banana instead. Serve with crusty bread and a leaf salad.

**1** Peel and dice the cucumber, then put in a sieve, sprinkle liberally with salt and leave to one side – the watery juices from the cucumber will be drawn out by the salt to make the cucumber crunchier.
**2** Mix the yogurt, mayonnaise, curry paste and chutney together in a bowl. Finely chop the ginger and add it to the bowl.
**3** Chop the chicken or turkey into bite-size pieces and stone and slice the peach or nectarine.
**4** Add the chicken or turkey and peach or nectarine to the curried mayonnaise with half the cashew nuts and half the fresh coriander and stir together.
**5** Rinse the cucumber to remove the salt, then pat it dry thoroughly with kitchen paper. Stir into the curried chicken mixture and season to taste.
**6** Spoon into a serving bowl or on to individual plates and scatter with the remaining coriander and cashews. Serve.

# TERIYAKI CHICKEN WITH ORIENTAL VEGETABLES

Time to make: 15 minutes
Time to cook: 15 minutes

Serves 2

**1 garlic clove**

**1 fresh red chilli**

**1 teaspoon grated fresh root ginger**

**2 tablespoons dark soy sauce**

**1 tablespoon sunflower oil**

**2 boneless chicken breasts**

*Oriental vegetables*

**1 carrot**

**1 leek**

**60 g (2 oz) mange-touts**

**1 tablespoon sesame oil**

**1 teaspoon sesame seeds**

**3 tablespoons dry sherry**

**1 teaspoon cornflour**

**extra dark soy sauce, optional**

Although you can buy teriyaki sauce, this home-made version is so quick to mix up, I think the extra five minutes in the kitchen is worth the effort – especially for the spicy fragrance the fresh ginger adds. I love the clean, lemony flavour of fresh root ginger and never buy the powdered variety, which to me tastes soapy by comparison. I even use fresh ginger in cakes! To serve with this Japanese-style dish I usually choose boiled rice or Chinese egg noodles.

**1** Crush the garlic into a shallow bowl. Halve, seed and thinly slice the chilli, then add to the bowl with the ginger, soy sauce and oil and mix together well.

**2** Add the chicken, turn it over in the soy mixture until well coated and leave to marinate until you are ready to cook; the longer the chicken marinates, the more flavour it will have.

**3** Meanwhile, prepare the Oriental vegetables. Peel, halve and shred the carrot. Trim, thoroughly rinse and shred the leek. Top and tail and shred the mange-touts. You should end up with long matchstick-like strands.

**4** About 5 minutes before you are ready to cook, preheat the grill.

**5** Remove the chicken from the marinade and place it on the grill rack; reserve the marinade.

**6** Grill the chicken for about 15 minutes, turning it over once, until it is tender and the juices run clear when it is pierced with the tip of a knife.

**7** While the chicken is grilling, cook the vegetables. Heat the oil in a wok or large frying pan over a high heat. Add the sesame seeds and stir-fry for a few seconds until they start to colour.

**8** Add the carrot and leek to the wok or pan and continue stir-frying for 3 to 4 minutes.

**9** Stir the sherry into the cornflour to make a smooth paste, then add it to the reserved marinade and stir together. Add to the vegetables, including the mange-touts, stirring until the mixture is bubbling. Taste and add a little extra soy sauce to the vegetables, if necessary. Transfer to a serving dish and serve at once.

# PARMESAN CHICKEN WITH RATATOUILLE

Time to make: 15 minutes
Time to cook: about 20 minutes

Serves 2

**1 courgette**
**1 small red pepper**
**½ aubergine**
**2 tablespoons olive oil**
**1 garlic clove**
**400 g (14 oz) can chopped tomatoes**
**30 g (1 oz) Parmesan cheese**
**2 boneless, skinless chicken breasts**
**8 fresh basil leaves**
**salt and freshly ground black pepper**
**extra fresh basil sprigs, to garnish**

*Parmesan Chicken with Ratatouille (front) with Mexican-style Chicken with Crisp Tortillas and Cheese, see page 16*

For something simple this is really rather special. When I first thought of coating chicken breasts with Parmesan cheese, I wasn't too sure how well the cheese would stick. I soon discovered, however, that the natural moisture on the outside of the chicken breasts makes the perfect adhesive, and if you use a non-stick pan, the result will be tender chicken with a crusty, cheesy coating that marries beautifully with the Mediterranean flavour of ratatouille. My husband and I enjoy this served with either mashed or new potatoes or buttered tagliatelle and a salad.

**1** Thinly slice the courgette, seed and slice the pepper and quarter and thinly slice the aubergine.
**2** Heat half the oil in a large saucepan over a medium heat. Crush the garlic, add it to the pan and fry for just a few seconds.
**3** Stir in the courgette, red pepper and aubergine and stir-fry for a few minutes, then add the tomatoes with their juice and plenty of seasoning.
**4** Cover the pan and allow the mixture to simmer gently for about 15 minutes while preparing and cooking the chicken.
**5** Grate the Parmesan cheese on to a plate, then press the cheese on to the outside of each chicken breast – it's important that the outside of the chicken is still quite moist, so don't pat it dry with kitchen paper first.
**6** Heat the remaining oil in a large non-stick frying pan over a high heat until hot. Add the chicken breasts and cook for about 10 minutes, turning them over once, until golden and crusty and the juices run clear when pierced with the tip of a knife.
**7** Shred the basil leaves and add them to the ratatouille. Spoon on to serving plates with the chicken and garnish with basil sprigs. Serve immediately.

# MEXICAN CHICKEN WITH CRISPY TORTILLAS AND CHEESE

Time to make: 10 minutes
Time to cook: about 20 minutes

Serves 2

**2 garlic cloves**
**1 onion**
**1 tablespoon olive oil**
**2 boneless, skinless chicken breasts**
**1 fresh green chilli**
**400 g (14 oz) can peeled tomatoes**
**1 teaspoon ground cumin**
**½ chicken stock cube**
**7 g (¼ oz) fresh coriander**
**30 g (1 oz) mature Cheddar cheese**
**40 g (1½ oz) tortilla chips**
**4 tablespoons soured cream**
**salt and freshly ground black pepper**

*Photographed on page 15*

The tortilla chips used to top this filling dish are the spicy triangular corn chips more usually served with drinks, but I like the texture and the extra spice they add to the topping. For casual parties, I've made large bowls of this and served it with rice, a salad and Re-fried Beans with great success. Yet, whatever quantity you make, I recommend that the tortillas go on at the last minute to stop them absorbing the juice from the chicken layer and becoming soggy. This doesn't really need anything more than boiled rice and a salad to make a delicious evening meal.

1 Chop or crush the garlic and halve and thinly slice the onion.
2 Heat the oil in a flameproof casserole or large saucepan over a medium heat. Add the garlic and onion, then fry, stirring occasionally, for 6 to 8 minutes until softened.
3 Meanwhile, cube the chicken and seed and thinly slice the chilli.
4 Add the chicken and chilli to the casserole or pan and stir-fry with the onion for about 3 minutes until the chicken changes colour.
5 Drain the tomatoes, reserving the juice, then add them to the pan with half their juice, the cumin, the crumbled stock cube and seasoning to taste. Simmer gently, uncovered, for about 10 minutes, stirring occasionally, until the chicken is tender. Add a little more tomato juice, if necessary, to moisten the mixture, but the consistency shouldn't be too wet or the tortillas will become soggy when they are added.
6 While the chicken is simmering, chop the coriander and grate the cheese. Preheat the grill to high.
7 Stir most of the fresh coriander into the mixture, then taste and adjust the seasoning if necessary.
8 If you haven't used a flameproof casserole, transfer the mixture to a flameproof serving dish. Scatter with the tortillas, then spoon over the soured cream, top with the grated Cheddar cheese and scatter over the remaining chopped coriander.
9 Grill until the top is bubbling and the cheese melts, checking regularly to ensure the tortillas don't 'catch'. Serve immediately.

# CHICKEN AND CHORIZO GUMBO

Time to make: 5 minutes
Time to cook: about 30 minutes

Serves 2

**1 tablespoon sunflower oil**
**4 boneless, skinless chicken thighs**
**1 onion**
**1 garlic clove**
**150 g (5 oz) chorizo sausages**
**1 green pepper**
**60 g (2 oz) fresh okra, optional**
**½ tablespoon plain flour**
**2 teaspoons ground coriander**
**1 teaspoon chilli powder**
**½ teaspoon ground turmeric**
**3 fresh bay leaves**
**230 g (7¼ oz) can chopped tomatoes**
**220 ml (7 fl oz) strongly flavoured chicken stock**
**salt and freshly ground black pepper**

Gumbo is a spicy American stew from the region around New Orleans thickened with the vegetable okra, which gives off a sticky juice as it cooks. Although gumbo is usually made with seafood, here I have combined chicken thighs with chorizo, a spicy Spanish sausage. The okra can be omitted if you find it difficult to track down in your area, and you can use French beans instead. Serve this in shallow bowls with boiled rice.

1 Heat the oil in a large saucepan or flameproof casserole over a high heat. Halve the chicken thighs, then add them to the pan and fry for about 5 minutes, stirring occasionally, until they start to brown.

2 While the chicken is frying, thinly slice the onion, crush the garlic and slice the chorizo sausage, green pepper and okra.

3 Add the onion and garlic to the pan as soon as they are prepared, then cook with the chicken until they are softened. Stir in the chorizo, green pepper and okra and continue cooking for a few minutes more.

4 Meanwhile, put the flour in a small bowl and blend with a little water to form a smooth paste, then set aside.

5 Stir the ground coriander into the pan with the chilli powder, turmeric, bay leaves and tomatoes with their juice, stirring until well blended.

6 Add the flour mixture, stock and seasoning to taste, stirring together well until thickened.

7 Cover and simmer, stirring occasionally, for 15 to 20 minutes until the chicken is tender and the juices from the chicken run clear when pierced with the tip of a knife. Serve immediately.

# PAN-COOKED CHICKEN WITH PEARS AND BACON

Time to make: 10 minutes
Time to cook: 20 to 25 minutes

Serves 2

**½ tablespoon sunflower oil**

**2 boneless chicken breasts**

**2 rashers smoked back bacon**

**1 onion**

**1 garlic clove**

**1 firm, ripe pear**

**315 ml (10 fl oz) dry cider or perry**

**1 teaspoon fresh thyme leaves**

**salt and freshly ground black pepper**

Apples are often used in savoury cookery, but I find firm pears, although less tart, equally delicious and an unusual change. Here they're combined with tender chicken, smoky bacon and cider, or if you prefer, perry, which is the pear equivalent. Serve this with creamy mashed potatoes and a lightly cooked vegetable, such as carrots, broccoli or peas.

**1** Heat the oil in a non-stick frying pan over a high heat. Add the chicken breasts and cook for about 5 minutes until golden on both sides.

**2** While the chicken is cooking, de-rind and chop the bacon (I find this easiest with scissors). Slice the onion, crush the garlic and peel, core and thickly slice the pear.

**3** Remove the chicken from the pan and set aside.

**4** Turn down the heat a little, then add the bacon, onion and garlic to the pan and fry, stirring occasionally, for 6 to 8 minutes until the onions are tender and beginning to turn golden.

**5** Pour in the cider and sprinkle in the thyme and seasoning, then return the chicken to the pan. Cover and cook for about 5 minutes.

**6** Add the pears to the pan, then continue cooking, uncovered, for about 5 minutes more until the chicken is tender and the juices run clear when pierced with the tip of a knife and the cider has reduced to make a light sauce. Serve immediately.

*Pan-cooked Chicken with Pears and Bacon*

# TURKEY WITH ALMONDS AND BOURBON SAUCE

Time to make: 15 minutes
Time to cook: about 10 minutes

Serves 2

- **250 g (8 oz) skinless, boneless turkey breast meat, see Cook's Tip, below**
- **30 g (1 oz) plain flour**
- **½ teaspoon grated nutmeg**
- **¼ teaspoon ground allspice**
- **good pinch cayenne pepper**
- **315 ml (10 fl oz) milk**
- **1 tablespoon sunflower oil**
- **½ chicken stock cube**
- **1 to 2 tablespoons bourbon or whisky**
- **30 g (1 oz) toasted flaked almonds**
- **salt and freshly ground black pepper**

A few years ago I was invited to Kentucky in America to see first-hand how bourbon, the local rye whisky, is made. Armed with several bottles on my return, I set to work in the kitchen and devised a number of sweet and savoury recipes flavoured with bourbon. This creamy, spicy sauce with strips of turkey is one of them and it transforms the often rather bland and flavourless meat into a speedy meal that is really tasty and tender. Of course, as not everyone has bourbon in their drinks cabinet, I've also tried this with Scotch whisky with good results. Mashed potatoes and sweetcorn with a green vegetable such as broccoli or Savoy cabbage are the ideal accompaniments.

**1** Cut the turkey into thin strips.
**2** Put the flour, seasoning, nutmeg, allspice and cayenne in a plastic food bag. Add the turkey and shake until the turkey strips are well coated in the flour mixture. Remove the turkey strips from the bag and blend any leftover flour with the milk.
**3** Heat the oil in a large non-stick frying pan over a high heat. Add the turkey strips and stir-fry for about 5 minutes until golden.
**4** Pour in the milk and crumble in the stock cube, then simmer, stirring occasionally, until the milk thickens into a smooth, creamy sauce.
**5** Stir in the bourbon or whisky and bring to the boil to boil off the excess alcohol. Toss in the flaked almonds and serve while they are still slightly crunchy.

**Cook's Tip**
Packets of turkey meat already cut into strips are sold at large supermarkets. Look in the fresh meat department for the product labelled as 'turkey breast stir-fry'. Chicken can also be used.

# CHICKEN WITH LIME PILAFF

Time to make: 10 minutes
Time to cook: 25 to 30 minutes

Serves 2

**1 tablespoon olive oil**
**2 boneless chicken breasts**
**2 small onions**
**4 green cardamom pods**
**1 lime**
**125 g (4 oz) basmati rice**
**500 ml (15 fl oz) hot chicken stock**
**pinch saffron strands**
**1 tablespoon clear honey**
**30 g (1 oz) sultanas**
**salt and freshly ground black pepper**
**30 g (1 oz) toasted flaked almonds**

*Photographed on page 23*

This is sweet, fragrant and tangy all in one. Basmati rice, although a little more expensive than American long grain, has an aromatic flavour that is especially compatible with spices such as cardamom. But take care as it can easily over-cook if you don't keep a close eye on it towards the end of the cooking time. If you want an accompaniment, all this needs is a crisp leaf salad, or lightly cooked cauliflower, mange-touts or green beans.

1 Heat the oil in a large non-stick frying pan or flameproof casserole over a high heat. Add the chicken, skin side down, and cook for about 5 minutes until golden.
2 Turn the chicken over and quickly seal the other side by cooking for a further 1 to 2 minutes.
3 While the chicken is cooking, slice the onions. Crush the cardamoms, remove the seeds and discard the pods. Grate the rind and squeeze the juice from the lime.
4 Remove the chicken from the pan and set aside.
5 Add the onions to the pan and fry for 6 to 8 minutes, stirring occasionally, until they are beginning to colour.
6 Tip in the rice and stir so all grains are well coated in oil. Stir in the stock, saffron, crushed cardamom seeds, honey, sultanas and lime juice. Reserve the lime rind.
7 Return the chicken to the pan and season to taste. Bring to the boil, then cover, turn down the heat and simmer gently for 10 to 15 minutes until both the rice and the chicken are cooked and tender and all the stock has been absorbed. The juices should run clear when you pierce the breasts with the tip of a knife.
8 Toss in the almonds, scatter with the lime rind and serve.

**Cook's Tip**
When pan-frying the chicken (or any other meat), if you occasionally press it down on to the base of the pan in steps 1 and 2, the skin will brown evenly and quickly.

# SESAME-COATED TURKEY WITH MANGO SALSA

Time to make: 20 minutes
Time to cook: 10 to 12 minutes

Serves 2

**1½ tablespoons sesame seeds**
**1½ tablespoons plain flour**
**½ teaspoon ground coriander**
**1 egg**
**2 large turkey breast fillets**
**1 tablespoon sunflower oil**
**salt and freshly ground black pepper**
**fresh coriander sprigs, to garnish**

*Mango salsa*

**1 large, firm ripe mango**
**½ avocado, optional**
**4 spring onions**
**1 small fresh red chilli**
**1 lime**
**2 tablespoons chopped fresh coriander**

This started off as a bit of an experiment after a meal at a friend's house and developed into this exotic-tasting salad. It's also good with plain grilled chicken. All this needs in the way of accompaniments is a green salad and boiled basmati rice.

**1** Mix the sesame seeds, flour, ground coriander and salt and pepper to taste on a plate or in a shallow bowl.
**2** Break the egg into another shallow bowl and beat with a little salt and pepper.
**3** Coat the turkey breasts first in the egg, then in the flour and sesame seed mixture, turning them until they are evenly covered.
**4** Heat the oil in a non-stick frying pan over a medium heat. Add the turkey breasts and fry for 5 to 6 minutes each side until golden, crispy and the juices run clear when they are pierced with the tip of a knife.
**5** While the turkey is cooking, make the mango salsa. Peel, stone and chop the mango, working over a bowl to catch any of the juice; add the flesh to the bowl. Peel, stone and dice the avocado, if using, and add to the bowl. Chop the spring onions and seed and finely chop the chilli, then place them in the bowl with the mango. Squeeze the juice from the lime and add it to the bowl with the chopped coriander and seasoning to taste. Stir together.
**6** Place the turkey on serving plates, add a spoonful of the mango salsa and garnish with fresh coriander sprigs.

*Sesame-coated Turkey with Mango Salsa (front) with Duck and Raspberry Salad (centre left), see page 24, and Chicken with Lime Pilaff, see page 21*

# ROAST DUCK AND RASPBERRY SALAD

Time to make: 30 minutes
Time to cook: 15 to 20 minutes

Serves 2

**2 small, boneless duckling breasts, or 1 large boneless duck breast**

**1 lime**

**1 tablespoon redcurrant jelly**

**1 tablespoon soy sauce**

*Dressing*

**1 tablespoon olive oil**

**1½ tablespoons redcurrant jelly**

**1 teaspoon dark soy sauce**

**salt and freshly ground black pepper**

*Salad*

**¼ head lollo biondo or other lettuce**

**¼ head radicchio**

**1 small avocado**

**2 spring onions**

**60 g (2 oz) fresh raspberries, or just-thawed frozen raspberries if fresh are out of season**

*Photographed on page 23*

If you're entertaining mid-week and you want something quick, impressive and delicious, make this main-course salad which easily multiplies for larger numbers. It doesn't really even need an accompaniment, although boiled new potatoes or warmed French bread may be appreciated by hungrier guests.

**1** Preheat the oven to 220C, 425F, Gas 7.
**2** If you are using a large duck breast, halve it at a slight angle.
**3** Heat a non-stick frying pan (there's no need to add oil) over a high heat until hot, then add the duck breasts, skin side down, and fry for a few minutes until brown – you'll find a lot of fat comes from the skin.
**4** Turn the duck breasts over and cook for just a few seconds or so to seal on the underside.
**5** Meanwhile, grate the rind and squeeze the juice from the lime. Mix the redcurrant jelly, soy sauce and half the lime rind together in a shallow bowl, then add the duck breasts and turn in the mixture until well coated. Reserve the lime juice.
**6** Arrange the duck, skin side up, on a wire rack set over a roasting tin, then roast them in the oven for 10 to 15 minutes; I prefer duck still slightly pink in the middle, so I only roast it for 10 minutes, but roast for the full time if you like yours well done.
**7** While the duck is roasting, make the dressing. Shake all the dressing ingredients together in a jar with the lime juice and remaining rind until well combined.
**8** Prepare the salad ingredients and place them in a bowl. Tear the lollo biondo and radicchio into bite-size pieces. Peel, stone and slice the avocado and chop the spring onions.
**9** Pour over the dressing and raspberries and gently toss together just as the duck is ready to come from the oven.
**10** Arrange the salad on one side of large dinner plates, then slice and fan the duck on the other side. Spoon any dressing left in the salad bowl over the duck and serve immediately.

# ROAST DUCK WITH HOI-SIN GRAVY

Time to make: 10 minutes
Time to cook: 10 to 15 minutes

Serves 2

**2 small boneless duckling breasts, or 1 large boneless duck breast**

**60 ml (2 fl oz) hoi-sin sauce**

**½ teaspoon cornflour**

**2 tablespoons medium-dry sherry or Marsala**

**sprigs of fresh flat-leaf parsley or coriander, to garnish, optional**

Although the gravy for this uses hoi-sin, the Chinese barbecue sauce, this isn't, in fact, a Chinese-tasting dish – the hoi-sin just adds a lovely rich and spicy flavour, ideal for serving with vegetables and potatoes.

**1** Preheat the oven to 220C, 425F, Gas 7.
**2** If you are using a large duck breast, halve it at a slight angle.
**3** Heat a small non-stick frying pan (there's no need to add oil) over a high heat until hot, then add duck breasts, skin side down, and fry for a few minutes until very brown – you'll find quite a lot of fat comes from the skin.
**4** Turn the duck breasts over and cook for just a few seconds or so to seal on the underside.
**5** Arrange the duck, skin side up, on a wire rack set over a roasting tin, then roast them in the oven for 10 to 15 minutes; I prefer duck still slightly pink in the middle, so I only roast it for 10 minutes but cook for the full time if you want it well done.
**6** While the duck is roasting, rinse out the frying pan. Measure the hoi-sin sauce into a measuring jug and make up to 155 ml (5 fl oz) with water.
**7** Blend the cornflour with the sherry or Marsala until smooth, then stir it into the hoi-sin mixture. Pour into the frying pan and cook, stirring, until thickened.
**8** Remove the duck from the oven and thinly slice it on a board. Pour the sauce on to dinner plates, then fan out the slices of duck on top. Garnish with the herbs, if liked, and serve immediately.

**Cook's Tip**

The secret to crispy duck skin is to sear the breasts first in a non-stick pan, which not only removes a lot of the fat from the duck skin but also seals in the juices, ensuring the meat is moist and meltingly tender.

# Lamb, beef and venison

You will find traditional recipes in this chapter, such as a cobbler and a tender lamb stew with dumplings, as well as the slightly more exotic and spicy dishes for when you're in the mood for something foreign. I'm a great fan of venison, and it can be substituted for beef in any of these recipes.

# LAMB AND VEGETABLE STEW WITH ROSEMARY DUMPLINGS

Time to make: 10 to 15 minutes
Time to cook: about 30 minutes

Serves 2

**375 g (12 oz) lean lamb neck fillet**

**½ tablespoon sunflower oil**

**2 leeks**

**2 carrots**

**2 potatoes**

**625 ml (20 fl oz) beef or lamb stock**

**2 fresh bay leaves**

**1 sprig fresh rosemary**

**½ teaspoon ground coriander**

**salt and freshly ground black pepper**

*Dumplings*

**90 g (3 oz) self-raising flour**

**½ teaspoon ground coriander**

**⅛ teaspoon baking powder**

**30 g (1 oz) vegetable suet**

**½ teaspoon chopped fresh rosemary**

This is one of my husband Graham's favourite recipes. It's hearty, warming and perfect for chilly winter evenings. Over the years I've reduced the amount of suet in the dumplings, as I'm careful about how much fat we eat, but tastewise you'd never know. Our friends are often surprised that a dish like this can be cooked in such a short time, but the secret is down to the cut of meat – lean lamb fillet which cooks quickly and is always tender.

**1** Cut the lamb into cubes, discarding any excess fat.
**2** Heat the oil over a high heat in a flameproof casserole, preferably one that is smart enough to put on the table and serve out of. Add the lamb and fry for a few minutes, stirring occasionally, until it is evenly brown.
**3** While the lamb is cooking, thoroughly rinse and slice the leeks, scrub and slice the carrots and scrub and slice the potatoes. Add the vegetables to the pan as they are ready.
**4** Pour in the stock, then add the bay leaves, rosemary and coriander. Season to taste, then cover and leave to simmer for about 20 minutes.
**5** While the lamb is simmering, make the dumplings. Sift the flour, coriander, baking powder and salt and pepper to taste into a bowl, then stir in the suet and rosemary.
**6** Stir in 4 tablespoons water and mix to make a fairly stiff dough. Cut the mixture into four and roughly shape into balls, then drop on top of the lamb stew. Cover again and leave to continue simmering for 5 minutes until the dumplings are risen, firm and cooked all the way through. Serve in soup bowls.

*Serving the dumplings and stew.*

# LAMB STEAKS WITH REDCURRANT AND ORANGE

Time to make: 5 minutes
Time to cook: 10 to 15 minutes

Serves 2

**2 lamb steaks or lamb chump chops, trimmed of all excess fat**

**1 small orange**

**2 tablespoons redcurrant jelly or rowanberry jelly**

**1 tablespoon whole-grain mustard**

**salt and freshly ground black pepper**

Orange isn't normally a flavour associated with lamb, but with whole-grain mustard and redcurrant jelly it makes a tasty basting sauce, while at the same time providing its own delicious gravy. A little fresh mint can be added if you have some, too. Serve these with new potatoes and stir-fried leeks, broccoli and carrots.

**1** Preheat the grill to high. Arrange the lamb steaks or chops in a flameproof dish.
**2** Grate a little of the rind and squeeze all the juice from the orange. Mix ¼ teaspoon of the orange rind with all the juice, the redcurrant jelly, mustard and salt and pepper to taste, then mash together with a fork to break up the jelly into the mixture.
**3** Pour the mixture over the lamb, then grill for 10 to 15 minutes, depending on the thickness of the lamb, so the steaks or chops are caramelized on the outside, but still moist and tender on the inside.

**Cook's Tip**
Some varieties of redcurrant jelly have quite a firm set, which makes them more difficult than others to mix into basting sauces and dressings. I find that a quick 'burst' in the microwave helps them dissolve more easily.

# PUBLICAN PIES WITH MUSTARD MASH

Time to make: 30 minutes, including boiling and mashing potatoes
Time to cook: about 25 minutes

Serves 2

**500 g (1 lb) large potatoes**
**1 Spanish onion**
**1 tablespoon sunflower oil**
**250 g (8 oz) lean minced lamb**
**1 tablespoon plain flour**
**155 ml (5 fl oz) stout**
**½ beef or lamb stock cube**
**1 tablespoon tomato purée**
**¼ teaspoon freshly ground black pepper, plus extra for seasoning**
**salt**
**15 g (½ oz) butter**
**2 teaspoons whole-grain mustard**
**2 teaspoons Dijon mustard**
**1 to 2 tablespoons milk**

When my husband and I want to eat something really savoury and satisfying, I invariably make this, which, I suppose, is a version of the classic Shepherd's Pie with the added richness and flavour of stout. Instead of adding vegetables to the meat mixture, however, I prefer to serve them separately, and tend to choose simple vegetables such as carrots and fresh peas or frozen petit pois when fresh are out of season.

1 Bring a large saucepan of salted water to the boil over a high heat. While the water is boiling, peel and cube the potatoes. Add the potatoes to the boiling water and boil for 15 to 20 minutes until very tender.
2 Meanwhile, chop the onion. Heat the oil in a non-stick saucepan over a medium heat. Add the onions and fry, stirring occasionally, for 8 to 10 minutes until softened and golden.
3 Stir in the lamb, using the spoon to break it up, and fry for about 5 minutes until it becomes brown and the mixture looks fairly juicy.
4 Stir in the flour, then blend in the stout and crumble in the stock cube. Stir in the tomato purée, pepper and a little salt. Allow to simmer for 10 minutes, stirring occasionally to prevent the mixture from sticking.
5 While the mince is cooking, preheat the grill.
6 Drain the potatoes, then return them to the pan and mash them thoroughly with the butter, both mustards, the milk and plenty of salt and pepper.
7 Spoon the lamb into a flameproof dish or 2 individual flameproof dishes and top with the mustard-flavoured mash. Grill for a few minutes until golden brown, then serve.

**Cook's Tip**
When I'm in a hurry to make mashed potatoes, I cube the potatoes very small to reduce the cooking time. However, the result is often slightly wetter, so mash first before adding any extra milk.

# LAMB SKEWERS WITH FRESH APRICOT TABBOULEH

Time to make: 25 minutes, including soaking wheat
Time to cook: 10 to 12 minutes

Serves 2

**1 tablespoon mint jelly**

**½ tablespoon Worcestershire sauce**

**375 g (12 oz) lean lamb neck fillet, all surplus fat removed**

**salt and freshly ground black pepper**

**fresh mint sprigs, to garnish**

*Apricot Tabbouleh*

**90 g (3 oz) bulgar wheat**

**250 g (8 oz) fresh apricots**

**4 spring onions**

**¼ cucumber**

**½ lemon**

**15 g (½ oz) fresh flat-leaf parsley**

**1 teaspoon ground coriander**

**60 g (2 oz) roasted, salted cashew nuts**

**2 tablespoons olive oil**

**4 tablespoons chopped fresh mint**

This recipe is for eating in the garden on a summer evening. It's full of summery flavours, yet at the same time cooling and refreshing. I based it on the traditional Middle Eastern cracked wheat dish, tabbouleh, adding tangy fresh apricots and roasted cashew nuts in place of the more usual tomatoes. Serve with warmed pitta or naan bread, which only takes seconds to warm through, so put it under the grill when you remove the skewers.

1 Put a kettle of water on to boil for the bulgar, and while you are waiting, stone and chop the apricots, finely chop the spring onions and dice the cucumber, adding each to a salad bowl as it is ready.
2 Once the water has boiled, put the bulgar in a separate heatproof bowl. Generously cover with the boiling water, then leave to soak for about 20 minutes.
3 Preheat the grill to high and line the grill pan with foil.
4 Mix together the mint jelly and Worcestershire sauce with some seasoning. Cube the lamb and stir into the mixture, making sure all the cubes are well coated. Thread onto skewers.
5 Place the lamb skewers on the grill rack and grill for 10 to 12 minutes, turning once until they are tender and beginning to char and caramelize.
6 While the lamb is grilling, finish the tabbouleh. Squeeze the juice from the lemon into the salad bowl with the apricots, spring onions and cucumber. Chop the parsley, then add it to the salad with the ground coriander, nuts and oil and stir together.
7 Drain the bulgar and squeeze out any excess moisture with your hands, then toss into the salad ingredients and season to taste. Mix together well and sprinkle with the chopped mint, then spoon on to serving plates and top with the lamb. I find it easiest to remove the skewers at this stage. Garnish with fresh mint and serve with warm bread.

*Lamb Skewers with Fresh Apricot Tabbouleh*

# LAMB AND ONION COBBLER

Time to make: 10 to 15 minutes
Time to cook: about 25 minutes

Serves 2

**1 large onion**
**1 garlic clove**
**1 tablespoon olive oil**
**250 g (8 oz) extra-lean minced lamb**
**½ tablespoon plain flour**
**¼ teaspoon salt**
**220 ml (7 fl oz) lamb or beef stock**
**1 tablespoon fresh thyme leaves**
**1 tablespoon Worcestershire sauce**
**freshly ground black pepper**

*Cobbler topping*

**125 g (4 oz) self-raising flour**
**¼ tsp salt**
**¼ tsp baking powder**
**30 g (1 oz) butter**
**1 egg**
**½ tablespoon milk**

A meat cobbler is quite an old-fashioned kind of dish, but when it's cold outdoors this is really satisfying and goes down well with my husband, Graham, who likes anything that looks vaguely like a pie! Serve with steamed cabbage or spinach and petits pois.

**1** Preheat the oven to 220C, 425F, Gas 7.
**2** Halve and thinly slice the onion and chop the garlic.
**3** Heat the oil in a saucepan over a medium heat. Add the onion and garlic and fry for about 10 minutes, stirring occasionally, until beginning to turn golden and caramelize.
**4** While the onions are cooking put the flour, salt, baking powder and butter for the cobbler topping in a food processor and blend for a few seconds to cut in the butter until the mixture looks like breadcrumbs.
**5** Now stir the minced lamb into the onions and cook over a high heat for a few minutes to brown. Sprinkle in the flour, stir well, then add all the remaining lamb ingredients. Leave to simmer for 5 minutes while finishing the cobbler topping.
**6** Turn on the food processor again and add the egg and milk to the flour and butter mixture and whiz together to make a soft dough.
**7** Turn the dough out of the food processor on to a clean lightly floured work surface and shape it into a small round cake. Cut into 4 to make triangular scones.
**8** Tip the mince mixture into a gratin dish, then arrange the scones on top. Bake in the oven for 10 minutes until golden.

# LAMB CUTLETS WITH STEM GINGER & CRANBERRY PILAFF

Time to make: 10 minutes
Time to cook: about 25 minutes

Serves 2

**1 onion**

**1 garlic clove**

**1 tablespoon sunflower oil, plus extra for brushing**

**½ teaspoon caraway seeds**

**125 g (4 oz) basmati rice**

**500 ml (15 fl oz) lamb, beef or vegetable stock**

**1 piece stem ginger**

**30 g (1 oz) dried cranberries**

**4 to 6 lean lamb cutlets**

**salt and freshly ground black pepper**

**flat-leaf parsley, to garnish**

Pilaffs are rather fashionable at the moment, although they've been a great favourite of mine for many years as they make a great change from potatoes. I've used cutlets here, but you can also make this with grilled chump chops or lamb fillet. Serve with green vegetables such as sugar snaps or mange-touts and broccoli or spinach.

**1** Preheat the grill to high.

**2** Thinly slice the onion and crush the garlic. Heat the oil in a large frying pan over a medium heat. Add the onions, garlic and caraway seeds and fry for 5 to 8 minutes until the onions have softened and are beginning to turn golden.

**3** Tip the rice into the pan, then stir so all the grains are well coated in the oil. Pour in the stock and grind in some salt and black pepper.

**4** Chop the ginger, then add to the pan along with the cranberries. Cover, turn down the heat and simmer for 12 to 15 minutes until the rice is just tender and the stock has been absorbed.

**5** While the pilaff is cooking, grill the lamb. Arrange the cutlets on the grill pan and brush with a little oil. Season to taste, then grill for 8 to 10 minutes, depending on how thick and meaty the cutlets are, until tender.

**6** Spoon the pilaff on to dinner plates, top with the cutlets and garnish with parsley.

### Cook's Tip

Dried cranberries are a relatively new ingredient to the UK, although they're extremely popular in the United States, where they're eaten straight from the bag as a snack as well as used in recipes in place of raisins or sultanas. Added to pilaffs, they give a wonderful sweet, yet slightly tart flavour, that works very well with plainly cooked lamb. Look for them in supermarkets and health food shops, but if you can't find any, substitute sultanas.

# TERIYAKI STEAKS WITH CHARRED ONION NOODLES

Time to make: 5 to 10 minutes
Time to cook: about 15 minutes

Serves 2

**3 tablespoons oyster sauce**
**3 tablespoons teriyaki sauce**
**2 fillet or sirloin steaks**
**1 cm (½ in) piece fresh root ginger**
**1 red onion**
**½ tablespoon sunflower oil**
**1 teaspoon sesame oil**
**125 g (4 oz) open cup mushrooms**
**7 g (¼ oz) fresh coriander**
**90 g (3 oz) medium egg thread noodles**
**1 tablespoon dry sherry**
**185 g (6 oz) fresh bean sprouts**

When my husband and I treat ourselves to a Chinese take-away and order chow mein, I like the pleasantly charred flavour of the stir-fried noodles. I've tried to re-create that flavour in this recipe by cooking the onions over a high heat until they start to caramelize. If you think one steak per person is a little extravagant, cut one into strips and stir-fry it with the mushrooms instead. This doesn't need much to accompany it – just some stir-fried peppers or broccoli.

**1** Mix the oyster and teriyaki sauces together in a shallow bowl. Add the steaks, then turn them over to ensure both sides are coated. Set aside.
**2** Preheat the grill and put a kettle of water on to boil for the noodles.
**3** Peel and cut the ginger into thin shreds. Halve and slice the onion to make chunky 'petals'.
**4** Heat the sunflower and sesame oils in a wok or large frying pan over a high heat. Add the ginger and onions and fry for 5 to 6 minutes, stirring occasionally, until charred.
**5** While the onions are frying, slice the mushrooms and roughly chop the coriander. When the water has boiled, place the noodles in a heatproof bowl, pour over the water, stir and leave to soak for about 5 minutes until they are just tender.
**6** Stir the mushrooms into the charred onions and fry for a few minutes more, stirring occasionally.
**7** Remove the steaks from the teriyaki sauce mixture, arrange on the grill pan and grill for 3 to 4 minutes on each side, depending on how well done you like your meat.
**8** Drain the noodles and set aside.
**9** Stir the sherry into the teriyaki sauce mixture left in the bowl, then pour into the onion mixture and toss in the bean sprouts. Stir-fry for about 30 seconds to heat through, then add the noodles and coriander. Toss until well coated and serve with the steaks.

*Teriyaki Steaks with Charred Onion Noodles (front) with Spicy Chilli Beef with Fresh Coriander,* *see page 36*

# SPICY CHILLI BEEF WITH FRESH CORIANDER

Time to make: 10 minutes
Time to cook: about 20 minutes

Serves 2

**1 onion**

**1 green pepper**

**1 tablespoon sunflower oil**

**1 garlic clove**

**250 g (8 oz) extra-lean minced beef**

**2 teaspoons ground coriander**

**2 teaspoons ground cumin**

**1 teaspoon dried crushed chillies**

**½ teaspoon dried oregano, or 1 teaspoon fresh chopped oregano**

**400 g (14 oz) can chopped tomatoes**

**1 beef stock cube**

**300 g (9½ oz) can red kidney beans, drained**

**7 g (¼ oz) fresh coriander**

**salt and freshly ground black pepper**

**extra fresh coriander, to garnish**

*Photographed on page 35*

In the evening, when my husband and I fancy a meal that's spicy, this is definitely one of our favourite dishes. I regularly make it in a huge vat and freeze the leftovers in packs of two portions ready to thaw and reheat at short notice in the microwave. I make a tomato, avocado and crispy lettuce salad, with finely chopped spring onions and a handful of raisins, and boil some long-grain rice to serve with this.

1 Thinly slice the onion and seed and finely dice the pepper.
2 Heat the oil in a saucepan over a medium heat. Crush the garlic into the oil, then add the onion and fry for 5 minutes until softened.
3 Stir in the mince with the spices and oregano and stir round the pan until well mixed, then stir in the tomatoes with their juice, the green pepper and the crumbled stock cube.
4 Stir in the drained red kidney beans and salt and pepper to taste, then cover and leave to simmer for 15 minutes, stirring occasionally.
5 While the mince mixture is cooking, chop the coriander. Stir into the mince mixture and serve, garnished with fresh coriander.

**Cook's Tip**
This spicy mince also makes a delicious filling for Mexican tacos, the crisp tortilla shells, topped with shredded lettuce and grated cheese.
To freeze, cool the mixture, then pack it into a freezer bag and label. Use within 3 months. To serve, thaw in the fridge overnight and reheat, or microwave from frozen until piping hot.

# STEAKS WITH MUSTARD MUSHROOMS

Time to make: 5 to 10 minutes
Time to cook: about 15 minutes

Serves 2

**30 g (1 oz) butter**

**1 garlic clove**

**2 venison or beef sirloin steaks**

**185 g (6 oz) open cup mushrooms**

**60 ml (2 fl oz) medium-dry sherry**

**1 tablespoon whole-grain mustard, see Cook's Tip, below**

**125 ml (4 fl oz) crème fraîche or soured cream**

**2 tablespoons chopped fresh parsley**

**salt and freshly ground black pepper**

**chopped fresh parsley, to garnish**

I quite often serve this on a Friday night to make a special start to the weekend, sometimes substituting pork steaks for the beef or venison. It also makes a quick, no-trouble dish if we have friends round mid-week. Serve with fresh tagliatelle and a salad.

**1** Melt the butter in a large non-stick frying pan over a high heat. Crush the garlic into the butter and stir it round the pan for a few seconds.

**2** Add the steaks, then fry them for 3 to 5 minutes on each side, depending on their thickness and how well done you like your meat. While the steaks are cooking, slice the mushrooms.

**3** Remove the steaks from the pan and set aside while making the sauce. Toss the mushrooms in the pan juices, stir-frying until they start to turn golden. Stir in the sherry and bubble rapidly until almost evaporated.

**4** Stir in the mustard, crème fraîche or soured cream, seasoning to taste and chopped parsley to make a creamy sauce.

**5** Return the steaks to the pan to heat through before serving, garnished with the parsley.

**Cook's Tip**

You'll find I use mustard quite a lot throughout this book. I particularly like whole-grain mustards but some brands are too vinegary or overpoweringly flavoured with cloves, so I make my own fairly mellow mustard. To make Honey-Garlic Mustard, soak 40 g (1½ oz) black mustard seeds and 40 g (1½ oz) white mustard seeds in warm water overnight. Drain and rinse them in a sieve (don't worry if they seem a little slimy). Tip the seeds into a food processor, then blend in 60 ml (2 fl oz) white wine vinegar, 2 tablespoons thick honey, 1 crushed garlic clove and 1 tablespoon salt. Spoon into a sterilized jar and store in the fridge.

# Pork and bacon

I'm often surprised how reasonably priced pork is compared with a lot of other meats, which makes it an ideal candidate for economical mid-week meals. This chapter includes recipes for pork in all its forms, from lean mince and chops to smoked bacon and sausages.

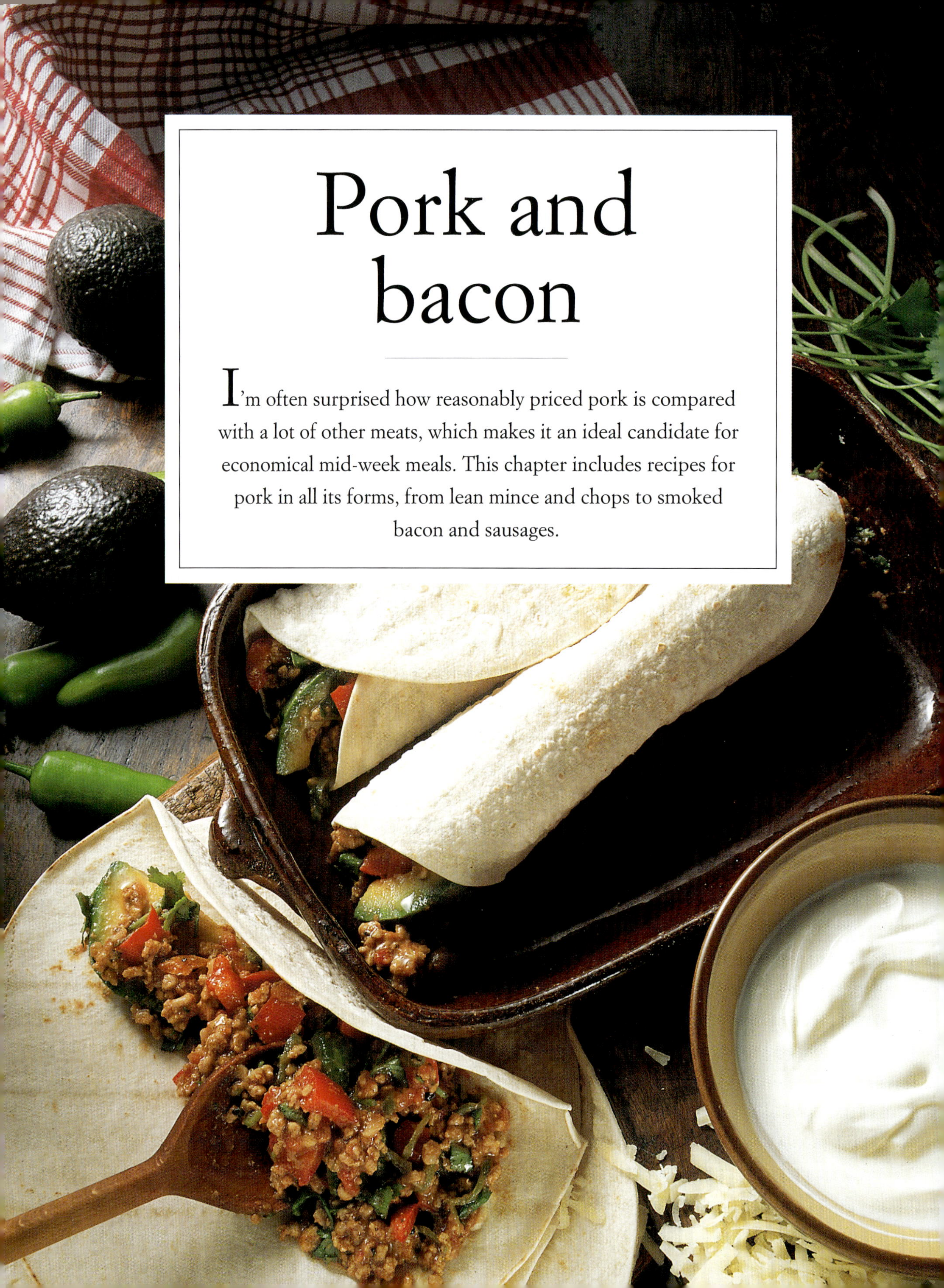

# ENCHILADAS WITH AVOCADO AND CHEESE

Time to make: 15 minutes
Time to cook: about 25 minutes

Serves 2

**2 fresh green chillies**
**1 red pepper**
**1 tablespoon sunflower oil**
**2 garlic cloves**
**250 g (8 oz) lean minced pork or beef**
**2 teaspoons each ground coriander and cumin**
**230 g (7½ oz) can chopped tomatoes**
**1 pork or beef stock cube**
**7 g (¼ oz) fresh coriander**
**1 avocado**
**60 g (2 oz) mature Cheddar cheese**
**4 soft tortillas**
**4 tablespoons crème fraîche or soured cream**
**salt and freshly ground black pepper**

Enchiladas are savoury Mexican pancakes made with soft tortillas, the traditional Mexican bread that forms the base of so many popular dishes like tacos and burritos. Soft flour tortillas can be bought ready-made from a growing number of supermarkets, and make a tasty supper stuffed with this spicy mince and avocado filling. I usually serve these with boiled long-grain rice, a tomato and onion salad and, if we're really hungry, a can of traditional Mexican Re-fried Beans.

**1** Seed and very finely slice the chillies, then core, seed and dice the pepper.
**2** Heat the oil in a large saucepan over a medium heat. Crush the garlic into the oil, then stir in the chillies, red pepper, mince, ground coriander and cumin. Stir round the pan until well mixed together, using the spoon to break up the mince.
**3** Stir in the tomatoes with their juice and crumble in the stock cube, then season to taste with salt and freshly ground black pepper.
**4** Bring to the boil, then cover, lower the heat and leave the mixture to simmer for 15 minutes, stirring occasionally.
**5** Meanwhile, chop the coriander and peel, stone and slice the avocado. Grate the Cheddar cheese.
**6** Preheat the grill to high while assembling the enchiladas.
**7** Stir the coriander and avocado into the mince mixture, then spoon it along the centre of each tortilla. Roll up like a pancake. Place in a gratin dish. Continue until all the mince mixture is used and you have filled all the tortillas; you can use individual flameproof dishes or one large one.
**8** Spoon over the crème fraîche and scatter with the grated cheese. Place under the grill and grill until golden and bubbling. Serve immediately.

*Filling the tortillas with the spicy mixture.*

# OVEN-ROAST PORK WITH MAPLE SYRUP AND MUSTARD

Time to make: 5 minutes
Time to cook: 20 to 25 minutes

Serves 2

**1 garlic clove**

**1 tablespoon maple syrup**

**1 to 2 teaspoons whole-grain mustard**

**1 tablespoon olive oil**

**250 to 375 g (8 to 12 oz) pork tenderloin**

**salt and freshly ground black pepper**

Whenever I serve this I'm ask for the recipe, yet it is so simple the only ingredient that I can put the secret down to is the maple syrup with its unique toffee flavour – honey is good, too, but maple syrup is definitely better. This is best served with plain vegetables like mashed potatoes, leeks and carrots.

**1** Preheat the oven to 200C, 400F, Gas 6.
**2** Crush the garlic into a bowl, then stir in the maple syrup, mustard, oil and plenty of seasoning.
**3** Cut the tenderloin in half if not already in 2 pieces, then put it into the bowl and turn until it is well coated on both sides.
**4** Place the tenderloin in an ovenproof dish and pour over any extra maple syrup mixture, then put it in the oven and roast for 20 to 25 minutes until it begins to caramelize on the outside and the juices run clear when you pierce the pork with the tip of a knife. Serve either in 2 large pieces or slice on a board before arranging on the plates.

**Cook's Tip**
Maple syrup is best known for serving American-style on pancakes and waffles, but the rich toffee flavour is scrumptious in biscuits and poured over vanilla ice cream, too. American settlers learnt from the Native Americans how to remove the sweet sap from the maple tree. They then boiled and concentrated the sap to produce the distinctive taste and rich colour that makes it so irresistible, as straight from the tree it is virtually tasteless. Although quite expensive, a little goes a long way.

# PORK STEAKS, CRÈME FRAÎCHE AND GREEN PEPPERCORNS

Time to make: 5 minutes
Time to cook: 10 to 15 minutes

Serves 2

**½ tablespoon sunflower oil**

**2 pork leg steaks or boneless pork chops**

**2 garlic cloves**

**1 tablespoon green peppercorns in brine, drained**

**125 ml (4 fl oz) dry white vermouth**

**90 ml (3 fl oz) strongly flavoured pork or chicken stock**

**155 ml (5 fl oz) crème fraîche or soured cream**

**1 tablespoon chopped fresh chives or parsley**

If you like peppered steaks, I think you'll like this version made with pork and best served with tagliatelle or new potatoes and a salad. Crème fraîche is a French cultured cream similar to soured cream, but creamier tasting. As well as using in savoury sauces like this, I also serve it with soft fruit in the summer and add it to mousses and cheesecakes. I also find dry vermouth an invaluable ingredient, and often use it in recipes rather than white wine to avoid having to open a bottle of wine for just a few tablespoons.

**1** Heat the oil in a non-stick frying pan over a medium heat. Add the pork and sear for 4 to 5 minutes each side until golden on the outside and almost cooked through. Remove from the pan and set aside.
**2** Crush the garlic and rinse and crush the green peppercorns and stir them into the pan. Stir in the vermouth, allowing it to bubble rapidly to boil off the alcohol and intensify its flavour.
**3** Stir in the stock, then quickly stir in the crème fraîche or sour cream to make a creamy sauce.
**4** Return the pork steaks or chops to the sauce to heat through and complete cooking; the juices should run clear if you pierce the meat with the tip of a knife.
**5** Stir in the chives or parsley and serve immediately.

**Cook's Tip**
Green peppercorns have a fresh, spicy flavour that is excellent in meat dishes like this, as well as stuffings – I often add a crushed teaspoon or two of the ones preserved in brine to the turkey stuffing at Christmas. Be warned, however, preserved peppercorns don't last indefinitely and can taste almost medicinal if they have been kept too long.

# PORK STEAKS WITH MARSALA, HAM AND CHEESE

Time to make: 5 minutes
Time to cook: about 15 minutes

Serves 2

**2 small boneless pork chump steaks**

**2 slices Gruyère cheese**

**2 slices Prosciutto di Speck or Parma ham**

**15 g (½ oz) butter**

**3 tablespoons Marsala, red vermouth or sweet sherry**

**salt and freshly ground black pepper**

**fresh flat-leaf parsley sprigs, to garnish**

This is a dish that's simple to make, yet tastes really special. I've based this on an Italian recipe which traditionally uses veal. I prefer not to eat veal, so pork makes a perfect substitute. Skinless, boneless chicken breasts can also be used. Serve with buttered fresh pasta, tossed with a few chopped fresh herbs, and a salad.

**1** Flatten the pork steaks by beating gently with a rolling pin, then top each one with a slice of Gruyère cheese and then the ham.

**2** Melt the butter in a large non-stick frying pan until sizzling. Add the pork, cheese and ham layers, pork side down, and cook, covered, for about 10 minutes. There's no need to turn the layers over while they cook.

**3** Pour in the Marsala, vermouth or sherry and season with salt and pepper, then cook, uncovered, for 5 minutes more until the cheese melts and the juices run clear when the pork is pierced with the tip of a knife.

**4** Transfer the pork layers to plates, spoon over the pan juices and garnish with the parsley. Serve immediately.

**Cook's Tip**

Prosciutto di Speck is a speciality ham from the Tyrol region of Italy. Similar in texture, but with a slightly smokier and more robust flavour, it's more economical than Parma ham for use in recipes like this. But when it comes to serving a slice of melon with ham, I will pay the extra for Parma ham.

*Pork Steak with Marsala, Ham and Cheese*

# GRILLED PORK WITH PLUM AND DAMSON SAUCE

Time to make: 5 to 10 minutes
Time to cook: 10 to 12 minutes

Serves 2

**2 boneless pork chump steaks or chops**

**sunflower oil for brushing**

**salt and freshly ground black pepper**

**chopped fresh parsley, to garnish**

*Plum and Damson Sauce*

**½ teaspoon cornflour**

**155 ml (5 fl oz) pork or chicken stock**

**2 tablespoons damson jam**

**1 teaspoon red wine vinegar**

**good pinch ground allspice**

**1 large plum**

Apple is more usually paired with pork, but the slightly tart flavour of fresh plum in this sauce with a little stock and the sweetness of damson jam produces a really quick and tasty alternative to serve with simply grilled pork steaks or chops. Creamy mashed potatoes, petits pois and leeks or broccoli are the perfect accompaniments for this dish.

In winter, when fresh plums are not available, or when I just want a quick no-fuss store cupboard sauce to make a change from gravy, I make this with just the jam.

**1** Preheat the grill to high.

**2** Meanwhile, brush both sides of the chops or steaks with a little oil, then season them with salt and pepper. Place the chops or steaks on the grill pan.

**3** Grill the pork for 5 to 6 minutes each side until tender and the juices run clear when the pork is pierced with the tip of a knife.

**4** While the chops are grilling, make the sauce. Put the cornflour into a small bowl. Blend a little of the stock into the cornflour until smooth, then stir in the remaining stock with the jam, vinegar and allspice.

**5** Pour this mixture into a saucepan and season to taste. Heat, stirring constantly, until bubbling and thickened and the jam has melted and is well blended.

**6** Stone and slice the plum, then stir it into the sauce and continue heating the sauce over a medium heat for about 2 minutes until the plum slices are softened but still retain their shape.

**7** Place the pork on serving plates and spoon over the sauce. Garnish with the parsley and serve.

# SMOKED PORK LOIN WITH ORCHARD SAUCE

Time to make: 10 minutes
Time to cook: about 20 minutes

Serves 2

**15 g (½ oz) butter**
**1 onion**
**1 dessert apple, such as Discovery or Cox**
**2 thick slices smoked pork loin or 2 lightly smoked sweet cure bacon chops**
**1 teaspoon plain flour**
**155 ml (5 fl oz) apple juice**
**1 teaspoon fresh chopped sage**
**freshly ground black pepper**
**fresh sage sprigs, to garnish**

Bacon often gets overlooked as a main dish ingredient, which is a shame. I really enjoy the savoury flavour of smoked pork loin and thick bacon rashers with this sweet apple sauce, although I sometimes use cider instead of apple juice, if it means specially buying the apple juice. Serve with mashed potatoes, leeks and petits pois or broccoli.

**1** Melt the butter in a non-stick frying pan over a medium heat. Meanwhile, slice the onion and core and slice the apple.
**2** If you are using bacon chops, snip the rind with scissors as this will stop them from curling in the pan. Add the pork or bacon to the pan and fry for about 2 minutes on each side. Remove from the pan and set aside.
**3** Add the onion to the pan and fry, stirring occasionally, for about 8 minutes until softened and beginning to turn golden.
**4** Mix the flour with a little water to make a smooth paste, then stir in the apple juice. Pour this mixture into the pan and stir to make a smooth sauce.
**5** Add the apple, sage and black pepper and leave to simmer for about 5 minutes, stirring occasionally but taking care that you don't break up the apple slices.
**6** Return the pork or bacon to the pan and heat through, then serve garnished with sprigs of sage.

**Cook's Tip**
I prefer the cloudy apple juices made from pressed English apples, rather than the thin, rather off-putting brown varieties. Many supermarkets now sell cartons of juice that state the variety of apple, such as Cox or Bramley, on the label. These are worth looking for, especially as you will be drinking what doesn't get used in the recipe.

# BOSTON BEANS WITH BANGERS AND BACON

Time to make: 5 minutes
Time to cook: about 25 minutes

Serves 2

**1 onion**

**1 bacon steak or 125 g (4 oz) smoked back bacon**

**1 tablespoon sunflower oil**

**250 g (8 oz) cocktail sausages**

**1 tablespoon cider vinegar, red wine or white wine vinegar**

**1 tablespoon Worcestershire sauce**

**400 ml (14 fl oz) passata**

**2 tablespoons dark brown sugar**

**2 tablespoons whole-grain mustard**

**1 teaspoon hot-pepper sauce**

**2 fresh or dried bay leaves**

**1 teaspoon fresh or ½ teaspoon dried thyme leaves**

**1 vegetable stock cube**

**432 g (14½ oz) can cannellini beans, drained**

**300 g (9½ oz) can red kidney beans, drained**

There's nothing subtle about this dish – it's tasty and gutsy, perfect for casual suppers and Firework Night. Serve it with boiled rice, baked potatoes (cooked in the microwave, then crisped up in the oven if religiously sticking to a 30-minute time limit) or hot garlic bread and a salad or coleslaw.

**1** Roughly chop the onion and de-rind and chop the bacon.
**2** Heat the oil in a large non-stick saucepan over a medium heat. Add the onions and fry for 3 to 5 minutes until softened.
**3** Add the sausages and bacon and continue frying for about 5 minutes more until the sausages are browned all over.
**4** Stir in the vinegar and allow it to sizzle (stand back or the fumes from the vinegar will make your eyes water), then stir in all the remaining ingredients.
**5** Simmer, uncovered, for 10 to 15 minutes, stirring occasionally, until rich and saucy. Serve at once.

**Cook's Tip**
Unless very young, bay leaves can be quite leathery, so it's a good idea to scrunch them in your hand before adding them to other ingredients to release their flavour and aromatic oils.

*Boston Beans with Bangers and Bacon*

# TOMATO RICE WITH CHEDDAR, LEEKS AND BACON

Time to make: 5 to 10 minutes
Time to cook: 20 to 25 minutes

Serves 2

**250 g (8 oz) leeks**

**1 garlic clove**

**125 g (4 oz) smoked back bacon rashers**

**1 tablespoon olive oil**

**125 g (4 oz) long-grain rice**

**230 g (8 oz) can peeled tomatoes**

**1 tablespoon whole-grain mustard**

**1 teaspoon sugar**

**500 ml (15 fl oz) vegetable stock**

**90 g (3 oz) mature Cheddar cheese**

**salt and freshly ground black pepper**

This is very much a store cupboard recipe – even when the fridge and larder are running low, I think most cooks can rustle together the few ingredients for this, although perhaps substituting onions for the leeks. Rather than grating the Cheddar I prefer to cut it into small cubes so they melt to make cheesy pockets of flavour amongst the other ingredients. Serve with something simple like steamed broccoli or a salad.

**1** Thoroughly rinse the leeks, then thinly slice them. Crush the garlic. De-rind and dice the bacon.

**2** Heat the oil in a large non-stick frying pan or flameproof casserole over a medium heat. Add the leeks, garlic and bacon and fry for about 5 minutes until they are beginning to soften and turn golden.

**3** Tip in the rice and stir round the pan until all the rice grains are coated in the oil and leek mixture, then stir in the tomatoes and their juice, breaking them down a little with a wooden spoon.

**4** Stir in the mustard, sugar and stock and season with plenty of black pepper – don't add salt yet as you may find when you taste it later that you don't need to use it, depending on how salty your bacon is.

**5** Cover, turn down the heat a little and leave to simmer for 15 to 20 minutes, stirring occasionally and adding a little water or more stock if necessary as the rice absorbs the tomato juice.

**6** While the rice is cooking, cube the cheese.

**7** Test the rice – it should be tender, but still slightly nutty in the centre – and decide whether you want to add salt. Toss in the Cheddar cheese, then serve.

# PORK AND CORN BURGERS WITH HOT TOMATO SAUCE

Time to make: 10 minutes
Time to cook: 12 minutes

Serves 2

**1 small onion**
**250 g (8 oz) extra-lean minced pork**
**90 g (3 oz) canned sweetcorn, drained**
**1 teaspoon ground coriander**
**¼ teaspoon salt**
**7 g (¼ oz) fresh coriander, optional**
**1 egg, beaten**
**2 slices of bread, about 60 g (2 oz)**
**1 tablespoon sunflower oil for frying**
**freshly ground black pepper**
**fresh coriander sprigs, to garnish**

*Hot Tomato Sauce*

**400 ml (14 fl oz) passata**
**60 ml (2 fl oz) strongly flavoured chicken stock**
**few drops hot-pepper sauce**
**1 garlic clove**
**1 tablespoon soft brown sugar**
**1 teaspoon ground coriander**

By 'hot' in this sauce, I mean flavour as well as temperature, although you can adjust or omit the hot-pepper sauce if you don't like your food too fiery. The fresh coriander isn't absolutely essential, unless, like me, you are addicted to its wonderfully aromatic flavour. I like to serve these with either boiled rice or new potatoes and lightly cooked fresh spinach.

1 To make the burgers, chop the onion and put it in a bowl with the pork, sweetcorn, ground coriander, salt and plenty of black pepper. Mix together with a wooden spoon until well combined.
2 Finely chop the fresh coriander, if using, then add half to the mixture with half of the egg. Mix again, this time squeezing the mixture with your hands if you don't mind getting messy.
3 Roughly tear up the bread, then put it in a food processor or blender and quickly process to make crumbs. Tip the crumbs out on to a plate, then pour the remaining egg into a soup plate.
4 Divide the pork mixture roughly into 4 portions, then firmly shape with your hands to make 'burgers' – the mixture will feel very soft and squidgy, but it will hold together once cooked.
5 Heat the oil in a large non-stick frying pan over a medium heat. Coat each burger first in the egg and then in the breadcrumbs, turning them so they are evenly coated. Place the burgers in the pan and fry for about 6 minutes on each side until golden and crispy; cook in batches if necessary.
6 While the burgers are frying, make the sauce. Put the passata, stock and hot-pepper sauce in a saucepan with the rest of the fresh coriander. Crush the garlic into the pan and add the sugar and ground coriander, then season with salt and pepper. Leave to simmer gently, stirring occasionally, until ready to serve.
7 Transfer 2 burgers to each serving plate, then spoon a little of the sauce over and garnish with the sprigs of coriander. Serve the remaining sauce separately.

# Fish and shellfish

Considering we live on an island it's amazing how little we eat fish in the UK, choosing it more often in restaurants than for cooking at home. But as it's so quick to prepare, it's an invaluable ingredient for the home-from-work cook, and it's a joy to eat when it's fresh.

# PIZZA-TOPPED COD

Time to make: 5 minutes
Time to cook: 10 to 12 minutes

Serves 2

**2 skinless, boneless cod fillets, thawed if frozen**

**2 tomatoes**

**4 slices Cheddar cheese**

**5 stoned black olives**

**salt and freshly ground black pepper**

As a small child I loathed cod, and it wasn't until I tried it with cheese that I grew to like it. This topping of Cheddar, tomatoes and olives is not only simple, but easy to rustle up from store cupboard ingredients if you already have cod fillets in the freezer. Serve with a salad and crusty bread or new potatoes and broccoli.

**1** Preheat the grill to medium.
**2** Arrange the cod fillets in a flameproof dish in a single layer, then grind over some seasoning.
**3** Slice the tomatoes, then arrange on top of the cod with the cheese slices.
**4** Halve or slice the olives and scatter them over the top.
**5** Place the dish under the grill and grill for 10 to 12 minutes until the cheese is golden and bubbling and the centre of the fish flakes when tested with a knife. Transfer to a plate and serve.

**Cook's Tips**
The tomatoes shield the heat from the fish, so it is important to give it a quick test in the centre to check it's cooked through before serving. Use the tip of the knife to test the flesh; if it is white and flaky, it is cooked through.
If you want to cook the cod fillets straight from the freezer, grill them for 5 minutes on each side before topping them with the cheese and tomatoes.

*Ready to serve tender cod fillets with melted cheese, tomato slices and olives.*

# SMOKED HADDOCK GRATIN WITH HORSERADISH

Time to make: 15 minutes, including 'poaching' the fish
Time to cook: 3 to 5 minutes

Serves 2

**375 g (12 oz) skinned smoked haddock fillet**
**90 g (3 oz) mature Cheddar cheese**
**30 g (1 oz) butter**
**30 g (1 oz) plain flour**
**315 ml (10 fl oz) milk**
**1 tablespoon mild horseradish sauce**
**salt and freshly ground black pepper**
**2 tomatoes**
**1 slice of bread**

We had fish for tea every other Saturday when I was a child. The choice was grilled herrings, cod or smoked haddock, and haddock was by far my favourite of the three. My father cooked the fish by pouring boiling water over and then just leaving it. If the water lost its heat before the fillets were ready, he would gently heat the water to simmering point on top of the gas and then leave it for a few minutes more. The result was really moist and flaky, so here I've used the same simple technique for this tasty supper dish with Cheddar cheese and horseradish. I like to serve this with mashed potatoes or crusty bread and a selection of green salad leaves with a vinaigrette dressing.

**1** Put a kettle of water on to boil. Halve the haddock, then put the fillets in a frying pan. Grate the cheese and set aside.
**2** Pour the boiling water over the haddock and leave the fish to 'poach' while making the sauce. Preheat the grill to high.
**3** Put the butter, flour, milk, horseradish sauce and salt and pepper to taste in a non-stick saucepan over a medium heat. Cook, stirring or whisking constantly, to make a thick, smooth sauce. Continue cooking gently for a few minutes so the flour doesn't taste raw, then remove from the heat and stir in two-thirds of the Cheddar cheese.
**4** Slice the tomatoes and dice the bread into small cubes. There is no need to remove the crusts unless they are very crispy.
**5** Drain the haddock, which should now be cooked through and will flake easily if you test it with the tip of a knife. If the fish isn't cooked through, gently bring the water up to the simmering point on top of the hob, then remove from the heat and leave for a few minutes more.
**6** Place the fish in a flameproof serving dish. Pour over the sauce and arrange the tomato slices in a row along the centre.
**7** Scatter the bread on either side of the tomatoes, then sprinkle the remaining grated Cheddar cheese over the top. Grill for 3 to 5 minutes until the topping is golden and crispy. Serve at once, straight from the dish.

# PAN-FRIED TROUT WITH LEMON AND ALMONDS

Time to make: 5 minutes
Time to cook: about 10 minutes

Serves 2

**2 gutted trout**
**3 to 4 tablespoons plain flour**
**1 lemon**
**30 g (1 oz) butter**
**30 g (1 oz) flaked almonds**
**salt and freshly ground black pepper**

Trout and toasted almonds are a classic combination and there have been many recipes based on this theme. This is a very simple version, and the only word of warning is to take care not to let the butter and almonds burn. In keeping with the classic simplicity of this dish, serve it with boiled potatoes and a mixed green salad.

**1** Snip the fins from the trout with scissors and cut off the head, if you want – I always remove it as otherwise the trout are usually too long for my frying pan, but the choice is yours.
**2** Mix the flour on a plate with salt and pepper to taste and squeeze the lemon juice into a shallow bowl.
**3** Melt the butter in a large non-stick frying pan over a medium heat. Dip the trout first in the lemon juice and then in the seasoned flour, turning them so they are evenly coated on both sides.
**4** Add the trout to the bubbling butter and fry for about 5 minutes over a medium to low heat until crispy.
**5** Turn the trout over and cook for another 5 minutes until that side is crispy, too. Scatter the almonds into the pan for the last few minutes so they brown in the buttery juices.
**6** Remove the trout from the pan and arrange on plates. Add the remaining lemon juice to the pan and stir well, then pour the pan juices and almonds over the fish. Serve immediately.

**Cook's Tip**
I particularly like the crisp cooked skin on trout and therefore always flour it before frying. To ensure the skin stays crispy after you've gone to so much trouble, don't add the lemon to the pan juices until the trout is out of the pan.

# SPICED SALMON WITH CHAR-GRILLED PEPPERS

Time to make: about 25 minutes, including grilling vegetables
Time to cook: 8 to 10 minutes

Serves 2

**1 large red pepper**
**1 large yellow pepper**
**olive oil for brushing and drizzling**
**1 garlic clove**
**125 g (4 oz) natural yogurt**
**1 teaspoon ground coriander**
**¼ teaspoon ground cumin**
**1 tablespoon fresh chopped dill**
**½ lemon**
**2 salmon steaks or cutlets**
**½ teaspoon crushed coriander seeds**
**salt and freshly ground black pepper**
**fresh dill sprigs, to garnish**

The spices in this are subtle enough not to overpower the flavour of the fish but still make it wonderfully aromatic. In the summer, I like to cook this on the barbecue for an even more char-grilled flavour. Serve with plain or spiced basmati rice and spinach stir-fried with a little fresh ginger, onion and whole cumin seeds.

1 Preheat the grill to high.
2 Quarter and seed the peppers, then put them on the grill rack, skin side up, and brush with oil. Grill for 15 minutes until they are quite blistered and charred all over.
3 While the peppers are grilling, crush the garlic and stir it into the yogurt with the coriander, cumin, dill and a squeeze of lemon juice. Season to taste with salt and pepper.
4 Spread the yogurt mixture on both sides of the salmon, then leave to marinate until the peppers are ready.
5 Remove the peppers from the grill rack and put the salmon in in their place. Grill for 8 to 10 minutes until cooked all the way through and the flesh flakes easily when tested with the tip of a knife. There is no need to turn the salmon over while it is grilling.
6 Meanwhile, peel the skins from the peppers, then slice them and place them in a bowl with the crushed coriander seeds, a drop of olive oil, a squeeze of lemon juice and salt and pepper to taste. Stir together well.
7 Serve the grilled salmon with the yogurt mixture, garnished with dill sprigs.

**Cook's Tip**
If you find the skins on grilled peppers are sometimes difficult to peel, try this: tip the peppers straight from the grill into a plastic food bag and seal, then leave for a few minutes while preparing another part of the meal. After about 5 minutes, the steam created from the heat of the peppers will have loosened the skins enough so that they peel away with no trouble at all.

*Spiced Salmon with Char-grilled Peppers served on saffron-flavoured rice with stir-fried spinach.*

# PLAICE ROLLS WITH GRUYÈRE AND CREAM

Time to make: 10 minutes
Time to cook: 15 minutes

Serves 2

**½ slice bread**

**2 whole plaice, filleted and skinned**

**90 ml (3 fl oz) double cream**

**60 g (2 oz) Gruyère cheese**

**salt and freshly ground black pepper**

**chopped fresh parsley, to garnish**

This is quite a mild flavoured dish, perfect for serving with grilled tomatoes, French beans and crusty bread. I always ask my fishmonger to fillet and skin the plaice so when I get home, this is literally in the oven within 10 minutes of starting.

**1** Preheat the oven to 200C, 400F, Gas 6.
**2** Tear the bread into pieces, then put it in a food processor or blender and process to make breadcrumbs. Alternatively, grate the bread – the result will be coarser but it saves on washing up!
**3** Make sure all the bones have been removed from the plaice fillets, then loosely roll up the fillets like a Swiss roll and arrange 2 fillets in individual gratin dishes or other ovenproof dishes. Season generously with salt and pepper.
**4** Spoon over the cream, then grate the cheese and sprinkle it on top of the cream.
**5** Scatter with breadcrumbs; you will need no more than about a tablespoonful for each dish.
**6** Put the dishes in the oven and bake for 15 minutes until the fish flakes easily when tested with the point of a knife and the tops are golden. Sprinkle with parsley and serve.

# CRAB CAKES WITH GUACAMOLE

Time to make: 15 minutes
Time to cook: 5 to 6 minutes

Serves 2

**two 185 g (6 oz) fresh dressed crabs, preferably from Cromer**

**3 tablespoons mayonnaise**

**2 spring onions**

**½ lime**

**100 g (3½ oz) fresh bread, about 3 slices**

**1 egg**

**1 tablespoon sunflower oil**

**salt and freshly ground black pepper**

**fresh coriander sprigs and lime wedges, to garnish**

*Guacamole*

**1 large ripe avocado**

**1 spring onion**

**1 tomato**

**1 tablespoon chopped fresh coriander**

*Photographed on page 2*

Ready prepared dressed Cromer crabs are widely available and make delicious crab cakes. I quite often serve these as a starter at dinner parties, making them ahead and then cooking them just before serving.

**1** Tip the crab meat into a bowl, then stir in the mayonnaise and salt and pepper to taste. Chop and add the spring onion and a squeeze of the lime juice, stirring gently to mix everything together well.
**2** Tear the bread into pieces, then put it in a food processor or blender and process to make coarse breadcrumbs.
**3** Add 45 g (1½ oz) of the breadcrumbs to the crab mixture, then stir to make a soft consistency. Do not worry if the mixture seems too soft, as it will firm up a little when cooked.
**4** Break the egg into a shallow bowl and beat with a fork, and tip the remaining crumbs into a soup plate.
**5** Divide the crab mixture into 4 portions and roughly shape into round cakes. Coat the crab cakes first in the egg and then the crumbs, pressing them on with your fingers.
**6** Heat the oil in a large non-stick frying pan over a medium heat. Add the crab cakes and fry for a few minutes on each side until crispy and golden. Don't be tempted to cook them too quickly or the outsides will burn before the centres heat through.
**7** While the crab cakes are frying, make the guacamole. Halve, stone and peel the avocado. Put the flesh in a bowl with the remaining lime juice and roughly mash together. Chop the spring onion and tomato, then add to the avocado mixture with salt and pepper to taste and chopped fresh coriander.
**8** Serve the guacamole with the crab cakes and garnish with coriander sprigs and lime wedges.

# BLACKENED FRESH TUNA WITH TOMATO SALSA

Time to make: 15 minutes
Time to cook: 10 minutes

Serves 2

**1 garlic clove**

**½ teaspoon salt**

**½ teaspoon ground coriander**

**½ teaspoon ground cumin**

**½ teaspoon dried chilli powder**

**1 tablespoon olive oil**

**2 fresh tuna steaks, see Cook's Tip, below**

**lime slices and fresh coriander sprigs, to garnish**

*Tomato Salsa*

**185 g (6 oz) cherry tomatoes**

**1 fresh green chilli**

**½ red onion**

**½ lime**

**7 g (¼ oz) fresh coriander**

**salt and freshly ground black pepper**

I first tasted fresh tuna on holiday in the Mediterranean. It was grilled over charcoal, and I've been a fan ever since. Tuna has a firm, flaky texture, more like meat than most fish, which marries well with spices and citrus flavours. Although referred to here as 'blackened', this doesn't mean that the fish is burnt. It's coated in spices and then pan-fried until quite dark and crusty on the outside, but still beautifully moist inside. As this is accompanied by a refreshing Mexican-style salsa, all you need to serve with it is some boiled American long-grain rice.

**1** Crush the garlic in a pestle and mortar with the salt, then stir in the ground coriander, cumin and chilli powder and oil.
**2** Rub the garlicky spice mixture on to both sides of the tuna.
**3** Heat a large non-stick frying pan over a high heat. Add the tuna and dry-fry, occasionally pressing down with a spatula, for 5 minutes, then turn over and dry-fry for 5 minutes on the other side until the flesh flakes easily when tested with the tip of a knife.
**4** While the tuna is cooking, make the salsa. Put all the ingredients in a bowl as you prepare them. Halve the cherry tomatoes. Seed and finely chop the chilli. Finely chop the red onion and squeeze the juice from the lime. Reserve 2 sprigs of coriander for a garnish, then chop and add the remainder to the bowl. Season with salt and pepper and stir together until well mixed.
**5** Spoon the salsa on to serving plates and serve with the blackened tuna. Garnish with the reserved coriander sprigs and lime slices, then serve.

**Cook's Tip**
Most good fishmongers and supermarkets now sell fresh tuna, although it's more usually bought frozen, if that isn't a contradiction. The portions vary quite dramatically in size depending on which part of the fish they come from and as it is a very meaty fish you will need to judge for yourself whether to serve one steak each or cut a large steak in half.

*Blackened Fresh Tuna with Tomato Salsa (front) with Malaysian Coconut Prawns and Cucumber, see page 60, served with Chinese noodles.*

BROS & SONS
ENGLAND
STAINLESS

# MALAYSIAN COCONUT PRAWNS AND CUCUMBER

Time to make: 15 minutes
Time to cook: about 10 minutes

Serves 2

- **½ cucumber**
- **1 onion**
- **2 garlic cloves**
- **1 fresh red chilli**
- **2 teaspoons ground coriander**
- **2 teaspoons ground cumin**
- **½ teaspoon fennel seeds**
- **½ teaspoon ground white pepper**
- **½ teaspoon ground turmeric**
- **1 tablespoon sunflower oil**
- **155 ml (5 fl oz) water, boiling**
- **60 g (2 oz) creamed coconut**
- **1 tablespoon fish sauce or light soy sauce**
- **1 tablespoon fresh lemon juice**
- **1 teaspoon soft brown sugar**
- **250 g (8 oz) extra-large cooked and peeled tiger prawns, thawed if frozen**
- **salt and freshly ground black pepper**

*Photographed on page 59*

Here's a great dish in its own right and for serving with noodles or boiled rice or as part of an Oriental menu when entertaining. (See my Cook's Tip, below.) Be sure the prawns just heat through in the sauce as they've already been cooked and will start to toughen if heated for too long.

**1** Peel and halve the cucumber, then cut away the seeds and cut the flesh into matchsticks. Spread out the cucumber on a plate, then sprinkle generously with salt and set aside while preparing the other ingredients. The salt will draw the excess moisture from the cucumber and give it a firmer texture.
**2** Finely chop the onion, cut the garlic into shreds and seed and very finely slice the chilli.
**3** Put the onion, garlic and chilli in a bowl, then stir in the ground coriander, cumin, fennel seeds, white pepper and turmeric.
**4** Heat the oil in a large non-stick frying pan over a medium heat. Add the onion and spice mixture and fry for about 3 minutes, stirring constantly to ensure the spices don't burn.
**5** Stir in the water and creamed coconut, stirring until it dissolves, then add the fish or soy sauce, lemon juice and sugar.
**6** Rinse the cucumber in a sieve under running water to remove the excess salt and shake dry, then add to the spicy coconut sauce and stir together.
**7** Stir in the prawns and heat through until bubbling. Serve at once.

**Cook's Tip**
For an Oriental menu to serve 6 guests, I often combine a couple of the recipes in this book, still sticking to the same quantities as you only need a few tablespoons of each dish served with boiled jasmine rice. This prawn dish goes well with the charred noodles (omit the steak in the recipe, or cut it into shreds and stir-fry with the mushroom) on page 34, Thai Chicken with Basil and Chillies, see page 11, and the Thai Vegetables with Satay Sauce and Lemon Grass, see page 89.

# PAN-COOKED PRAWNS WITH GINGER AND CORIANDER

Time to make: 10 minutes
Time to cook: about 6 minutes

Serves 2

**4 garlic cloves**

**60 g (2 oz) butter**

**2 teaspoons grated fresh ginger**

**1 teaspoon finely chopped fresh green chilli**

**4 tablespoons milk**

**4 tablespoons chopped fresh coriander**

**250 g (8 oz) raw headless king prawns or peeled cooked tiger prawns**

**freshly ground black pepper**

*Photographed on page 3*

On a sailing holiday in Turkey with friends, a local fisherman tied his boat alongside ours in bad weather and we spent an unusual evening demonstrating in sign language how most of the gadgets on our boat worked. At dawn he invited us on to his boat and we spent a memorable few hours watching him pull his nets. Offered first choice of his meagre catch, we bought a small bagful of huge blue-grey prawns and cooked them in garlic butter for lunch, which we then enjoyed with local bread and a salad. They were delicious and I certainly haven't eaten prawns as fresh since. But rather than just give a recipe for prawns in garlic butter, this is a way for zipping up a bag of large tiger prawns with fresh ginger and coriander. And you have a choice – buy them raw, still in their shells and eat with your fingers, or use a bag of peeled, cooked prawns so they just need to be heated through. I think prawns in their shells add much more flavour to the buttery sauce and pulling them from the shells is all part of the fun.

**1** Crush the garlic into a large frying pan over a medium heat. Add the butter, ginger and chilli and cook gently for about 2 minutes, stirring until the ginger and garlic are softened and beginning to turn golden.
**2** Add the milk, stirring quite quickly to make a creamy consistency, then stir in the coriander.
**3** Add the prawns and grind in some black pepper. If using raw prawns, cook for 1 to 2 minutes until they change from blue-grey to pink. If using ready-cooked prawns, simply stir until heated through.
**4** Serve the prawns in their shells with crusty bread and a side salad.

**Cook's Tips**

The peeled prawns and the sauce are also delicious served on buttered noodles.

If you are using ready-cooked prawns, take care to cook them gently and quickly so they don't toughen.

# Risottos, pizzas and pastas

Fresh or dried, there's something wonderfully satisfying about pasta. Creamy Italian risottos are equally rewarding, but not as yet as well known. And, of course, there are pizzas, another Italian favourite. This chapter provides you with delicious recipes for all three.

# FRESH ASPARAGUS AND PINE NUT RISOTTO

Time to make: 10 minutes
Time to cook: about 25 minutes

Serves 2

**1 tablespoon extra virgin olive oil**

**30 g (1 oz) pine nuts**

**1 onion**

**1 garlic clove**

**30 g (1 oz) butter**

**30 g (1 oz) fresh Parmesan cheese**

**185 g (6 oz) arborio rice**

**625 to 750 ml (20 to 25 fl oz) vegetable stock, boiling**

**100 g (3½ oz) asparagus tips, see introduction**

**90 ml (3 fl oz) dry white wine or dry white vermouth**

**salt and freshly ground black pepper**

**extra grated Parmesan, to serve, optional**

Small packets of asparagus sprue, the thin short stems of asparagus, are available for most of the year now and while not as luxurious as the wonderful thick home-grown stems that appear in May and June, they make a delicious addition to this risotto. I've also made this with trimmings of asparagus stems (although not the very ends which can be rather woody), making up the weight with French beans with good results. Serve with a salad and crusty bread. This is also delicious as a side dish with grilled chicken.

**1** Heat the oil in a large non-stick saucepan over a low heat. Add the pine nuts and fry, stirring frequently, until they are golden.
**2** While the pine nuts are frying, finely chop the onion and crush the garlic.
**3** Remove the pine nuts from the pan with a slotted spoon and set aside. Add the butter to the pan and melt. Add the onion and garlic and fry for 6 to 8 minutes until they are soft and beginning to turn golden.
**4** While the onions are frying, grate the Parmesan cheese.
**5** Tip the rice into the pan, then stir so all the grains are well coated in the buttery mixture.
**6** Pour half the hot stock into the pan and allow to bubble gently, stirring frequently, until absorbed.
**7** Add the rest of the stock a little at a time, stirring constantly, and simmer until the rice is almost tender and most of the stock is absorbed; you may not need to use all of the stock. Meanwhile, cut the asparagus into short lengths.
**8** Add the asparagus and pine nuts, then pour in the wine or vermouth. Continue simmering for about 5 minutes, stirring constantly, until the mixture achieves the classic creamy consistency and the rice and asparagus are tender. Stir in the cheese and serve, handing round more Parmesan if liked.

*Adding wine to the tender rice, asparagus and golden pine nuts.*

# FRESH SPINACH AND SUN-DRIED TOMATO RISOTTO

Time to make: 10 minutes
Time to cook: about 25 minutes

Serves 2

- **1 onion**
- **1 garlic clove**
- **1 tablespoon extra virgin olive oil**
- **30 g (1 oz) butter**
- **30 g (1 oz) fresh Parmesan cheese**
- **6 sun-dried tomatoes in oil, drained**
- **155 g (5 oz) arborio rice**
- **625 to 750 ml (20 to 25 fl oz) vegetable stock, boiling**
- **1 tablespoon pesto sauce, shop bought or see page 80**
- **200 g (7 oz) fresh young spinach leaves**
- **salt and freshly ground black pepper**
- **extra grated Parmesan cheese, to serve**

This is a great dish for vegetarians. I find that most of my 'veggie' friends long for really savoury and satisfying dishes, and this fulfils both criteria.

1 Finely chop the onion and crush the garlic.
2 Heat the oil and butter in a large non-stick saucepan over a medium heat. Add the onion and garlic and fry for 6 to 8 minutes, stirring occasionally, until softened and beginning to turn golden.
3 While the onions are frying, grate the Parmesan cheese and roughly chop the sun-dried tomatoes.
4 Tip the rice into the pan, then stir so all the grains are well coated in the buttery mixture.
5 Pour half the hot stock into the pan, then add the sun-dried tomatoes and pesto sauce and allow to bubble gently, stirring occasionally, until absorbed.
6 Add the rest of the stock a little at a time, stirring constantly, and simmer until the rice is tender; you may not need to add all the stock.
7 Stir in the spinach, season and continue cooking for about one minute until wilted, stirring constantly until the mixture achieves the classic creamy consistency.
8 Stir in the fresh Parmesan cheese and serve, handing round extra Parmesan.

**About Risottos**

I love rice of any description, whether as an accompaniment or as a main course, like these Italian-style risottos made with arborio rice. The variety of the rice is essential to the finished consistency, which should be moist and creamy – Italians say it's more like a soup than a rice dish. However, this is a speeded-up version of the classic recipe. Instead of adding the hot stock a tablespoon at a time and stirring constantly, as is traditional, I add half the stock in one go and only stir constantly towards the end of the cooking time. This way I can get on and prepare the rest of the meal! Arborio rice, or risotto rice, as it's also known, is sold in most large supermarkets and delis so don't be tempted to substitute another variety or you'll be disappointed with the result.

# PRAWN AND PARMESAN RISOTTO

Time to make: 10 minutes
Time to cook: about 25 minutes

Serves 2

**a good pinch of saffron threads**

**625 to 750 ml (20 to 25 fl oz) fish or chicken stock, boiling**

**1 onion**

**2 garlic cloves**

**30 g (1 oz) butter**

**1 tablespoon extra virgin olive oil**

**30 g (1 oz) fresh Parmesan cheese**

**185 g (6 oz) arborio rice**

**90 ml (3 fl oz) dry white wine or dry white vermouth**

**200 g (7 oz) peeled frozen prawns, thawed and drained**

**2 tablespoons chopped fresh parsley**

**salt and freshly ground black pepper**

**extra grated Parmesan cheese, to serve, optional**

This is delicious, but the secret is to add the prawns at the very last moment so they just heat in the risotto, as they quickly toughen if allowed to boil. You can use ordinary small Mediterranean prawns here, which means you get a prawn in every mouthful, or the larger tiger prawns if you prefer a more 'meaty' result.

**1** Stir the saffron into the boiling stock and leave to infuse so it releases its flavour and colour.
**2** While the saffron is infusing, finely chop the onion and crush the garlic.
**3** Melt the butter with the oil in a large non-stick saucepan over a medium heat. Add the onion and garlic and fry for 6 to 8 minutes, stirring occasionally, until softened and beginning to turn golden.
**4** Meanwhile, grate the Parmesan cheese.
**5** Tip the rice into the pan, then stir so all the grains are well coated in the buttery mixture.
**6** Gradually pour half the hot stock into the pan and season, then allow to bubble gently, stirring occasionally, until absorbed.
**7** Pour in the remaining stock a little at a time and continue simmering, stirring constantly, until the rice is tender; you may not need to add all the stock.
**8** Stir in the wine or vermouth and continue stirring until the mixture achieves the classic creamy consistency.
**9** Stir in the prawns, parsley and freshly grated Parmesan cheese, making sure the mixture doesn't boil or the prawns will toughen and spoil. Serve, handing round more Parmesan if liked.

**Cook's Tip**
You need hot stock to make risottos, so if you are using fresh stock bring it to the boil in a saucepan or in a microwave before you start. If you make up stock cubes with boiling water, the stock will be at the correct temperature.

# MUSHROOM AND SMOKED BACON RISOTTO

Time to make: 15 minutes
Time to cook: about 25 minutes

Serves 2

**30 g (1 oz) butter**

**250 g (8 oz) button mushrooms**

**1 onion**

**2 garlic cloves**

**1 tablespoon extra virgin olive oil**

**125 g (4 oz) smoked bacon, diced**

**185 g (6 oz) arborio rice**

**625 to 750 ml (20 to 25 fl oz) vegetable stock, boiling**

**45 g (1½ oz) fresh Parmesan cheese**

**90 ml (3 fl oz) dry white wine or dry white vermouth**

**2 tablespoons chopped fresh parsley**

**salt and freshly ground black pepper**

**extra grated Parmesan cheese, to serve, optional**

For a really deep mushroom flavour, I sometimes add a few dried mushrooms, such as ceps, to this dish. There's no need to soak them first, unless they are gritty – just snip them into pieces with scissors and add to the pan at the beginning of cooking.

**1** Melt the butter in a large non-stick saucepan over a medium heat. Slice the mushrooms, then add them to the pan and fry until they begin to turn golden.
**2** While the mushrooms are frying, finely chop the onion and crush the garlic.
**3** Remove the mushrooms from the pan with a slotted spoon and set aside. Add the oil to the pan and heat, then add the onion, garlic and bacon and fry, stirring occasionally, for about 8 minutes until soft and beginning to turn golden.
**4** Tip the rice into the pan, then stir so all the grains are well coated in the buttery mixture.
**5** Pour half the stock into the pan and allow to bubble gently, stirring occasionally, until absorbed.
**6** Meanwhile, grate the Parmesan cheese.
**7** Pour in the rest of the stock a little at a time and continue simmering, stirring constantly, until all the rice is tender; you may not need to add all the stock.
**8** Gradually add the wine or vermouth, stirring constantly, until the mixture achieves the classic creamy consistency.
**9** Stir in the sautéed mushrooms and any juices with the parsley and grated Parmesan cheese and serve, handing round more Parmesan if liked.

*Mushroom and Smoked Bacon Risotto*

# SIMPLE SCONE PIZZA BASE AND TOMATO TOPPING

Time to make: about 10 minutes
Time to bake: about 15 minutes

Serves 2

*Scone Pizza Base*

**250 g (8 oz) self-raising flour**
**½ teaspoon baking powder**
**pinch of salt**
**60 g (2 oz) butter**
**155 ml (5 fl oz) milk**
**flour for dusting**
**olive oil for brushing**

*Quick Tomato Sauce*

**230 g (7½ oz) can chopped tomatoes**
**1 large garlic clove**
**1 tablespoon sun-dried tomato paste, optional**
**pinch sugar**
**salt and freshly ground black pepper**

I often use different varieties of bread as the base for pizzas, such as Indian naans, Middle Eastern pittas, English muffins, thick horizonal slices of French bread or Italian ciabatta. However, this store cupboard 'scone' base, which I've used for the following five recipes, takes some beating. It's light, very quick to whizz together in the food processor and is in the oven within minutes of starting. While your pizza is baking, throw together a mixed salad or a bowl of chunky coleslaw.

1 Preheat the oven to 220C, 425F, Gas 7 with a large baking sheet inside.
2 To make the scone pizza base, put the flour, baking powder, salt and butter in a food processor and whizz together until the mixture looks like fine breadcrumbs.
3 Quickly whizz in the milk to make a soft dough, then turn it out on to a lightly floured work surface – the mixture will be quite sticky, but don't worry as it will soon come together once you start kneading it.
4 Gently shape the dough into a ball, then roll it out into a 25 cm (10 inch) circle. Lift on to the hot baking sheet and brush with a little olive oil.
5 Bake in the oven for 5 minutes.
6 While the pizza base is baking, make the quick tomato sauce. Mix together all the sauce ingredients.
7 Remove the pizza base from the oven and spread the sauce on top. Quickly scatter with your chosen topping ingredients (make your selection from the ideas on the following pages) and return the pizza to the oven for 10 to 15 minutes, depending on your choice of topping.

**Cook's Tip**
If you don't like your pizzas too tomato-tasting, leave out the tomato sauce and instead use a light spreading of pesto sauce, see page 80, or sun-dried tomato paste or olive paste. As well as spreading on to pizza bases, I add sun-dried tomato paste to salad dressings, soups and sauces to enrich the flavour.

# BLT PIZZA

Time to make: about 10 minutes
Time to cook: 15 to 20 minutes

Serves 2

**4 to 6 rashers smoked back bacon, de-rinded**

**1 quantity scone pizza base, see page 68**

**1 quantity quick tomato sauce, see page 68**

**2 tomatoes**

**90 g (3 oz) mild Cheddar or Edam cheese**

**freshly ground black pepper**

**90 g (3 oz) Iceberg lettuce**

**mustard-flavoured mayonnaise, to serve**

Here is a pizza and salad in one, inspired by the classic American BLT sandwich made with crispy bacon, lettuce and tomatoes. The lettuce isn't baked. Instead, it's shredded and then piled on top of the pizza at the last minute with mustard-flavoured mayonnaise.

**1** Preheat the grill to high and preheat the oven to 220C, 425F, Gas 7 with a large baking sheet inside.
**2** Put the bacon under the grill and grill while making the scone pizza base dough. Roll out the dough into a 25 cm (10 inch) circle, place it on the baking sheet and bake for 5 minutes.
**3** While the pizza base is baking, drain the bacon on kitchen paper, then cut each rasher into 3 pieces. Make up the quick tomato sauce. Slice the tomatoes and cheese.
**4** Remove the pizza base from the oven and spread with the tomato sauce, then top with the tomato slices, cheese and bacon pieces. Grind some fresh pepper over the top.
**5** Return the pizza to the oven to bake for a further 10 minutes until the cheese has melted.
**6** While the pizza finishes baking, shred the lettuce. Remove the pizza from the oven and pile the lettuce on top, then spoon the mustard-flavoured mayonnaise on top. Serve at once.

# SPICY PEPPERONI PIZZA WITH CHILLIES AND OLIVES

Time to make: about 10 minutes
Time to bake: 15 to 20 minutes

Serves 2

**1 quantity scone pizza base, see page 68**

**1 quantity quick tomato sauce, see page 68**

**125 g (4 oz) mozzarella cheese, drained**

**2 fresh green chillies**

**90 g (3 oz) pepperoni slices**

**8 to 10 stoned black olives**

**freshly ground black pepper**

**fresh oregano, optional**

This is one of my favourite pizzas as the combination of pepperoni sausage and fresh chillies makes it quite hot and spicy. Omit one or both of the chillies if you prefer a milder version.

**1** Preheat the oven to 220C, 425F, Gas 7 with a large baking sheet inside.
**2** Make up the scone pizza base dough, roll it out into a 25 cm (10 inch) circle, place it on the baking sheet and bake for 5 minutes.
**3** While the pizza base is baking, make the quick tomato sauce. Slice the mozzarella cheese. Seed and thinly slice the chillies.
**4** Remove the pizza base from the oven and spread with the sauce. Scatter over half the pepperoni slices, cover with the mozzarella cheese slices and chillies and then top with the remaining pepperoni slices and olives. Grind some fresh pepper over the top.
**5** Return the pizza to the oven to bake for a further 10 to 15 minutes until the topping starts to brown.
**6** Remove the pizza from the oven, sprinkle with oregano, if using, and serve.

**Cook's Tip**

Pepperoni is an Italian sausage made from a mixture of coarsely chopped pork and beef and seasoned with a mixture of spices, the most obvious being paprika. Packets of ready-sliced pepperoni are sold in most supermarkets. If you buy yours from a deli, ask to have it thinly sliced by machine to save you time once you get home.

*Spicy Pepperoni Pizza with Chillies and Olives (front) with Chicken Tikka Pizza with Fresh Coriander, see page 72.*

# CHICKEN TIKKA PIZZA WITH FRESH CORIANDER

Time to make: about 15 minutes
Time to bake: 10 to 15 minutes

Serves 2

**1 tablespoon tikka paste**

**2 tablespoons natural yogurt**

**½ tablespoon sunflower oil**

**2 boneless, skinless chicken breasts**

**1 quantity scone pizza base, see page 68**

**1 quantity quick tomato sauce, see page 68**

**125 g (4 oz) mozzarella cheese, drained**

**3 spring onions**

**¼ teaspoon cumin seeds**

**freshly ground black pepper**

**3 tablespoons chopped fresh coriander**

*Photographed on page 71*

As a fan of Indian food, I think this makes a great-tasting pizza sprinkled with aromatic fresh coriander. I often use naan bread for this recipe instead of the scone base, and you can use chicken tikka pieces from the supermarket if you don't want to start from scratch.

**1** Preheat the grill to high and preheat the oven to 220C, 425F, Gas 7 with a large baking sheet inside.
**2** Put the tikka paste, yogurt and oil in a bowl and mix together, then chop the chicken breasts, add them to the bowl and turn them over to coat in the mixture.
**3** Put the chicken under the grill and grill for 5 minutes, turning the pieces over once, until the juices run clear when they are pierced with the tip of a knife.
**4** While the chicken is grilling, make up the scone pizza base dough, roll it out into a 25 cm (10 inch) circle, place it on the baking sheet and bake for 5 minutes.
**5** While the base is baking, make the quick tomato sauce. Slice the mozzarella cheese and chop the spring onions.
**6** Remove the pizza base from the oven and spread with the sauce, then scatter the chicken and spring onions over the top and cover with the mozzarella cheese. Sprinkle with cumin seeds and black pepper.
**7** Return the pizza to the oven to bake for a further 5 to 10 minutes until the cheese melts.
**8** Remove the pizza from the oven, scatter with fresh coriander and serve.

# HAM AND SPINACH PIZZA

Time to make: about 10 minutes
Time to bake: about 20 minutes

Serves 2

**1 quantity scone pizza base, see page 68**

**1 quantity quick tomato sauce, see page 68**

**60 g (2 oz) young spinach leaves**

**125 g (4 oz) mozzarella cheese, drained, or mild Cheddar cheese**

**125 g (4 oz) wafer-thin smoked ham slices**

**1 tablespoon capers, drained**

**2 eggs**

**freshly ground black pepper**

Lightly baked eggs and capers add extra flavours that are not always expected on pizzas. The eggs are broken on top at the last minute and then the whole pizza is put back in the oven until the eggs are lightly set. I like the extra tang capers add, but feel free to omit them if you're not fond of the flavour.

**1** Preheat the oven to 220C, 425F, Gas 7 with a large baking sheet inside.
**2** Make up the scone base dough, roll it out into a 25 cm (10 inch) circle and turn up the edge to make a lip all around. Place it on the baking sheet and bake for 5 minutes.
**3** While the pizza base is baking, make the quick tomato sauce. Shred the spinach and slice the cheese. Rinse the capers if you do not want them to be too strong tasting (see Cook's Tip, below).
**4** Remove the pizza base from the oven and spread with the sauce. Pile the spinach on top, then cover with the ham, sprinkle with the capers and top with the cheese. Grind some fresh pepper over the top.
**5** Return the pizza to the oven to bake for a further 10 minutes until the cheese has melted.
**6** Remove the pizza from the oven and break an egg on each half, then return it to the oven for at least 5 minutes until the eggs are lightly set. Serve at once.

**Cook's Tip**
If you dislike capers because they are too vinegary, rinse them well under cold water and you will be surprised at the difference.

# THREE-CHEESE PIZZA WITH FRESH BASIL

Time to make: about 10 minutes
Time to bake: 10 to 15 minutes

Serves 2

**1 quantity scone pizza base, see page 68**

**1 quantity quick tomato sauce, see page 68**

**60 g (2 oz) Red Leicester or Cheddar cheese**

**60 g (2 oz) Crottin de Chaignol or other goats' cheese**

**60 g (2 oz) dolcelatte or other blue cheese**

**freshly ground black pepper**

**fresh basil leaves**

Quite simply, this is delicious. And, it's a good way of using up leftover bits of cheese. In fact, you don't have to stop at three cheeses – simply use up anything that's too small to put out on a cheeseboard.

**1** Preheat the oven to 220C, 425F, Gas 7 with a large baking sheet inside.
**2** Make up the scone pizza base dough, roll it out into a 25 cm (10 inch) circle, place it on the baking sheet and bake for 5 minutes.
**3** While the pizza base is baking, make the quick tomato sauce. Slice the cheeses.
**4** Remove the pizza base from the oven and spread with the sauce. Top with the cheeses, then grind over some black pepper. Return the pizza to the oven to bake for a further 5 to 10 minutes until the cheese has melted.
**5** Remove the pizza from the oven, scatter with fresh basil leaves and serve.

**Cook's Tip**
When topping the pizza with the different cheeses, dot them around, rather than concentrating them in areas, to get a variety of flavours on every slice.

*Three-cheese Pizza with fresh basil*

# PASTA SPIRALS WITH CHEESE AND MUSHROOMS

Time to make: 10 minutes
Time to cook: about 20 minutes

Serves 2

**155 g (5 oz) dried pasta spirals**

**15 g (½ oz) butter**

**250 g (8 oz) mushrooms, either one variety such as button or chestnut, or a mixture**

**155 ml (5 fl oz) milk**

**125 g (4 oz) garlic-and-herb flavoured soft cheese**

**2 tablespoons chopped fresh flat-leaf parsley**

**salt and freshly ground black pepper**

**flat-leaf parsley sprigs, to garnish**

Most soft cheeses will melt when gently warmed to make an instant sauce for pasta, so it's always worth keeping a tub of one in the fridge for when you want a no-fuss supper. Here I've used garlic-and-herb flavoured cheese with some sliced mushrooms, although you can easily adapt this to whatever you have – try smoked ham or crispy bacon with quickly sautéed peppers and broccoli. To complete the meal, all you need is a fresh spinach salad and crusty bread.

**1** Bring a large saucepan of salted water to the boil, then add the pasta spirals and cook according to the packet instructions until just tender, which should be about 20 minutes.
**2** While the pasta is boiling, melt the butter in a large saucepan over a high heat. Slice the mushrooms, add them to the pan and fry for about 5 minutes, stirring occasionally, until they are beginning to turn golden.
**3** Stir in the milk and cheese, then lower the heat and cook, stirring constantly, to make a smooth, creamy sauce.
**4** Drain the pasta and immediately stir it into the sauce. Add black pepper, salt and parsley and toss until all the spirals are well coated in the sauce. Spoon on to plates and garnish with parsley sprigs. Serve immediately.

**Cook's Tip**
Pasta is ready to eat when it's al dente – tender but still with a bit of a bite. The only way you can really tell is to try a piece; it should be firm without any taste of flour or crunch.

# SMOKED SALMON AND PASTA WITH VODKA AND DILL

Time to make: 8 minutes
Time to cook: about 5 minutes

Serves 2

**185 g (6 oz) fresh fettuccine, preferably one flavoured with black pepper**

**125 g (4 oz) smoked salmon or trout**

**155 ml (5 fl oz) double cream**

**1 tablespoon chopped fresh dill**

**2 tablespoons vodka**

**salt and freshly ground black pepper**

**fresh dill sprigs, to garnish**

*Photographed on page 79*

I first tasted this when my friend Julia, the Art Director of *Living,* cooked supper on a location photography trip, and it has been a favourite of mine ever since. It's unbelievably simple, glamorous enough for instant entertaining and delicious. To set off the flavours, serve this with a salad that includes some slightly bitter leaves, such as chicory or frisée. I also sometimes serve it with steamed broccoli and crusty bread.

**1** Bring a large saucepan of salted water to the boil, then add the fettuccine and boil according to the packet instructions until just tender, which should be about 5 minutes.
**2** While the fettuccine is boiling, cut the salmon into long shreds with scissors, then set aside.
**3** Mix together all the remaining ingredients in a saucepan over medium heat and stir until gently boiling and slightly thickened.
**4** Drain the pasta, then add it with the salmon to the sauce and toss together until all the fettuccine is well coated.
**5** Transfer to serving bowls, garnish with fresh dill and serve at once.

**Cook's Tip**
If you don't have any fresh dill, substitute 2 tablespoons snipped fresh chives or spring onion tops instead.

# RAVIOLI WITH SUN-DRIED TOMATOES AND CHILLI

Time to make: 5 minutes
Time to cook: about 15 minutes

Serves 2

**250 g (8 oz) fresh ravioli, such as the ones filled with chicken, mortadella and Parmesan, or any other filled pasta of your choice**

**2 garlic cloves**

**1 fresh green chilli**

**6 sun-dried tomatoes in oil, drained**

**1 tablespoon olive oil, or use the oil from the sun-dried tomatoes**

**400 g (14 oz) can chopped tomatoes**

**185 g (6 oz) fresh young spinach leaves**

**salt and freshly ground black pepper**

**flat-leaf parsley sprigs, to garnish, optional**

*Ravioli with Sun-dried Tomatoes and Chilli (back) with Smoked Salmon and Pasta with Vodka and Dill (front), see page 77, and Fresh Spaghetti with Home-made Pesto, see page 80.*

This rich tomato sauce is also perfect for tossing with other fresh filled pastas, such as tortellini and cappelletti. Sun-dried tomatoes are available from both delis and large supermarkets and add an extra depth of flavour. For an authentic accompaniment, pick up a loaf of Italian ciabatta or focaccia bread when you are at the supermarket, or keep a supply of the excellent part-baked breads in your freezer. I usually serve this with a crisp leaf salad, into which I slice an avocado.

**1** Bring a large saucepan of salted water to the boil, then add the ravioli and cook according to the instructions on the packet, which should be about 15 minutes.
**2** While the ravioli is boiling, crush the garlic and seed and finely chop the chilli. Roughly chop the sun-dried tomatoes.
**3** Heat the oil in a medium-sized saucepan over a medium heat. Add the chilli and garlic and briefly fry until softened, but not golden.
**4** Stir in the sun-dried tomatoes and the canned tomatoes with their juice and season to taste, then simmer gently, uncovered, for about 5 minutes, stirring occasionally.
**5** Roughly chop the spinach, then add it to the pan, stirring until it is wilted. Leave the sauce to bubble gently to make a thick sauce.
**6** Drain the pasta, then toss into the sauce and serve, garnished with parsley, if liked.

**Cook's Tip**
Spinach can often be quite gritty and time-consuming to prepare, so save time by buying packets of young leaves at the supermarket, as they are already rinsed and ready to use.

# FRESH SPAGHETTI WITH HOME-MADE PESTO

Time to make: 5 minutes
Time to cook: 5 to 7 minutes

Serves 2

**185 g (6 oz) fresh spaghetti**

**salt and plenty of freshly ground black pepper**

**extra grated Parmesan cheese, to serve**

*Pesto Sauce*

**30 g (1 oz) fresh Parmesan cheese**

**15 g (½ oz) fresh basil leaves and stems**

**2 garlic cloves**

**¼ teaspoon salt**

**3 to 4 tablespoons extra virgin olive oil**

**3 tablespoons pine nuts**

*Photographed on page 79*

Pesto is well known as a fragrant sauce for pasta, and although there are some very good shop-bought varieties around, I regularly make my own, particularly in the summer when I have a good supply of home-grown basil. It keeps well in the fridge and is brilliant for flavouring many other dishes, such as vegetable soups and pizza bases, or for stuffing under the skin of roast chicken. Although many recipes suggest grinding the ingredients by hand in a pestle and mortar, I think a short whizz in the food processor is much more convenient – and the result just as good. Serve with a tomato salad and some good crusty bread.

**1** Bring a large pan of salted water to the boil, then add the spaghetti and boil according to the packet instructions until just tender, which should be 5 to 7 minutes.
**2** While the spaghetti is boiling, make the pesto sauce. Roughly grate the Parmesan cheese. Set aside a few basil leaves, then put the rest in a food processor with the garlic, salt, olive oil and pine nuts and whizz together until fairly smooth.
**3** Drain the pasta and immediately return it to the pan over medium heat. Toss in the pesto and stir until all the spaghetti is well coated.
**4** Transfer to serving plates, garnish with the reserved basil leaves and serve with extra cheese for sprinkling over the top.

**Cook's Tip**
This recipe makes enough pesto sauce for one pasta meal, but you can double the quantities and put the remainder in a jar, as it keeps really well in the fridge for at least a week. The pesto is also perfect to use in Fresh Spinach and Sun-dried Tomato Risotto on page 64.

# FRESH TAGLIATELLE WITH TWO MUSTARDS AND SMOKED HAM

Time to make: 5 minutes
Time to cook: about 7 minutes

Serves 2

**185 g (6 oz) fresh tagliatelle**
**125 g (4 oz) wafer-thin smoked ham**
**3 spring onions**
**60 ml (2 fl oz) milk**
**60 g (2 oz) mayonnaise**
**1 teaspoon English mustard**
**1 heaped teaspoon whole-grain mustard**
**salt and freshly ground black pepper**

You'll probably be surprised to find milk and mayonnaise used for the base of this quick pasta dish, but I find they're the perfect everyday ingredients for making a creamy sauce for ham, tuna, and salmon pasta dishes when I don't have any time to shop for fresh cream – and the sauce really works. Look for American-style smoked ham at the supermarket because it's really thin and smoky. I serve this with a simple cucumber salad and crusty Granary bread.

**1** Bring a large saucepan of salted water to the boil, then add the tagliatelle and boil according to the packet instructions until just tender, which should be about 5 minutes.
**2** While the tagliatelle is boiling, roughly shred the ham and chop the spring onion. Mix them together in a bowl with all the remaining ingredients, stirring until well blended.
**3** Drain the pasta and immediately return to the pan with the other ingredients and heat gently, tossing the mixture together until the pasta is well coated in the sauce and the sauce has heated through. Serve.

**Cook's Tips**
Here I've added English and whole-grain mustards to flavour the creamy sauce, but try experimenting with combinations of your own, such as fresh herbs with tuna and capers or lemon rind and a squeeze of juice, or a few green olives with a can of salmon. For a lower-fat version, use a reduced-calorie mayonnaise with skimmed milk.

# Vegetarian main dishes

I'm not a vegetarian, but there are definitely occasions when I don't want to eat meat. My only stipulation is that the dishes must be full of flavour, but with the wide choice of fruit and vegetables in the shops and the opportunity to enjoy so many different cuisines, that side of the bargain is easy.

# POTATO, GINGER AND ONION ROSTIS WITH MINT RAITA

Time to make: 10 minutes
Time to cook: 15 to 18 minutes

Serves 2

**500 g (1 lb) potatoes**
**1 onion**
**1 teaspoon cumin seeds**
**1 teaspoon ground coriander**
**1 teaspoon turmeric**
**½ teaspoon salt**
**2 teaspoons grated fresh root ginger**
**4 tablespoons chopped fresh coriander**
**3 to 4 tablespoons sunflower oil**

*Mint Raita*

**1 tablespoon mint jelly**
**100 g (3½ oz) Greek-style yogurt**
**salt and freshly ground black pepper**

Whenever we go out for an Indian meal my huband, Graham, always orders onion bhajis. He can't resist them! So this recipe is a cross between potato bhajis and crispy Swiss potato cakes, rostis. The rostis are accompanied by a mint raita so all that's needed to serve with them is a refreshing salad.

**1** Peel and grate the potato into a bowl, then finely chop the onion and add it to the bowl. Stir in the spices, salt, fresh ginger and chopped coriander.
**2** Heat the oil in a large non-stick frying pan over a medium heat. Shape the potato mixture into 6 balls, then fry them in the hot oil, flattening the rostis against the pan with a fish slice.
**3** Cook gently for 8 to 10 minutes until crisp and golden, then turn the rostis over and cook the other side for 5 to 8 minutes more until crisp and golden. If you have 2 frying pans it's quicker to use both at the same time or you'll have to fry the rostis in batches.
**4** While the rostis are frying, make the raita. Mix the mint jelly into the yogurt and season to taste.
**5** Serve the rostis with the raita.

**Cook's Tips**
Rostis rely on the starch in the potatoes to bind them together, so don't be tempted to rinse the potatoes once they are grated. It's also important not to cook them too quickly or the outsides will burn before the centres are cooked through.

*Turning a rosti so it is crisp and golden on both sides.*

# CREAMY CAULIFLOWER AND COCONUT CURRY

Time to make: 10 minutes
Time to cook: 20 to 25 minutes

Serves 2

**1 onion**
**1 large garlic clove**
**2 fresh red chillies**
**1 tablespoon sunflower oil**
**1 tablespoon finely chopped fresh root ginger**
**2 teaspoons black mustard seeds**
**1 teaspoon each ground coriander, cumin and turmeric**
**½ teaspoon salt**
**freshly ground black pepper**
**500 ml (15 fl oz) vegetable stock**
**125 g (4 oz) creamed coconut**
**1 cauliflower**
**60 g (2 oz) sultanas**
**432 g (14½ oz) can chick-peas, drained**
**1 teaspoon garam masala, see Cook's Tip, opposite**

I often cook this as a vegetable dish to accompany an Indian menu, or as a meal in its own right, served with basmati rice, chutneys and naan bread or poppadoms. It makes a great change from the more traditional cauliflower cheese.

**1** Slice the onion, crush the garlic and seed and thinly slice the chillies.
**2** Heat the oil in a large saucepan over a medium heat. Add the onion, garlic and ginger and fry, stirring occasionally, for 6 to 8 minutes until softened and beginning to turn golden.
**3** Stir in the chillies, mustard seeds, spices, salt and black pepper, then pour in the stock and add the coconut. Stir until smooth.
**4** Cut the cauliflower into small florets, then add to the pan with the sultanas and chick-peas. Stir well, cover the pan and simmer for 15 to 20 minutes until the cauliflower is just tender.
**5** Just before serving, stir in the garam masala.

**Cook's Tip**
Garam masala is a blend of ground aromatic spices usually containing cinnamon, cardamom, black peppercorns, cloves and cumin. Because of its fragrant nature it is added towards the end of cooking, or literally sprinkled over the food as it's served, to preserve its flavour – you'll find it in the spice section of most supermarkets.

# TWO-CHEESE SPINACH BAKE

Time to make: 10 minutes
Time to cook: 15 minutes

Serves 2

**250 g (8 oz) young leaf spinach**

**60 g (2 oz) mature Cheddar cheese**

**125 g (4 oz) cottage cheese**

**3 eggs**

**1½ teaspoons ready-made English mustard**

**good grating fresh nutmeg**

**salt and freshly ground black pepper**

This is similar to the filling of a quiche or a Spanish omelette, packed with lots of fresh spinach and flavoured with mature Cheddar cheese and mustard. The second cheese in this recipe is cottage cheese which I'm normally not that keen on, but it's perfect in this. Serve with a fresh tomato and onion salad and crusty bread.

**1** Preheat the oven to 190C, 375F, Gas 5.
**2** Put the spinach in a non-stick saucepan over a medium heat, then cover and cook for just 1 to 2 minutes until wilted, stirring regularly. If you are worried that the mixture might catch, add a tablespoon of water.
**3** Grate the Cheddar cheese into a bowl, then stir in the cottage cheese, eggs, mustard, nutmeg and salt and pepper to taste, beating until well blended.
**4** Squeeze any excess moisture from the spinach, then roughly chop and add to the egg mixture.
**5** Divide the mixture between 2 greased 315 ml (10 fl oz) ovenproof dishes and bake for 15 minutes until set and beginning to turn golden. Serve immediately.

# WARM FETA AND TOMATO SALAD WITH AVOCADO

Time to make: 20 minutes
Time to cook: 5 minutes

Serves 2

**125 g (4 oz) cherry tomatoes**

**¼ frillice or Iceberg lettuce, see Cook's Tip, below**

**2 spring onions or a little sweet red onion**

**1 firm, ripe avocado**

**10 fresh mint leaves**

**1 garlic clove**

**½ lemon**

**1 tablespoon clear honey**

**½ teaspoon whole-grain mustard**

**3 tablespoons plain flour**

**½ teaspoon ground cumin**

**freshly ground black pepper**

**175 g (6 oz) feta cheese**

**2 to 3 tablespoons olive oil**

*Warm Feta and Tomato Salad with Avocado (back) with Char-grilled Vegetables with Basil Butter Sauce (front), see page 88, and Thai Vegetables with Satay Sauce and Lemon Grass, see page 89, served with boiled rice.*

Feta, the crumbly, salty Greek cheese, is delicious in this salad, coated first in cumin-spiced flour and then quickly fried until golden and crispy on the outside, but soft and melting inside. This also makes a good starter for summer barbecues followed by lamb kebabs or a herby chicken dish.

**1** Prepare the salad ingredients, putting them in a bowl as they are ready. Halve the cherry tomatoes, tear the lettuce into pieces and chop the spring onions. Peel, stone and slice the avocado and chop the mint. Toss together.
**2** Crush the garlic, then put it in a shallow bowl. Squeeze in the lemon juice and add the honey and mustard.
**3** Mix the flour, cumin and black pepper together on a plate. Thickly slice the cheese, taking care not to let the slices crumble, then coat them in the spiced flour mixture, making sure they are covered on all sides.
**4** Heat the oil in a non-stick frying pan over a high heat. Add the flour-coated cheese slices and fry quickly until golden and crispy. Turn over and cook for a few minutes more.
**5** Arrange the cheese on top of the salad leaves. Pour the dressing into the pan and quickly swirl round until heated through. Pour over the salad and serve immediately.

**Cook's Tips**

I also make this with haloumi, the more 'rubbery' cheese from Cyprus, with excellent results, and it's slightly easier to fry if you are worried that the feta may break up – the secret I find is to ensure the oil is really hot so the flour virtually browns on impact with the pan.

Frillice is a semi-hearted frilly version of an Iceberg lettuce, with the same crisp juicy leaves. If you can't find it, substitute another crisp lettuce, such as Iceberg or Cos.

# CHAR-GRILLED VEGETABLES WITH BASIL BUTTER SAUCE

Time to make: 10 minutes
Time to cook: 15 to 20 minutes

Serves 2

**1 small aubergine**

**2 courgettes**

**1 large red pepper**

**2 tablespoons olive oil**

**500 ml (15 fl oz) vegetable stock**

**185 g (6 oz) bulgar wheat**

**2 tablespoons white wine vinegar**

**30 g (1 oz) butter**

**10 fresh basil leaves**

**salt and freshly ground black pepper**

*Photographed on page 87*

The flavours of Mediterranean vegetables such as aubergine, peppers and courgettes really intensify when they are grilled. As well as serving them in this recipe, I sometimes grill the same combination of vegetables with fresh plum tomatoes and garlic and then toss them into pasta with fresh basil and cubes of Edam or mozzarella cheese. Serve this on its own or with a side salad and crusty bread.

**1** Preheat the grill to high.
**2** Slice the aubergine lengthways, slice the courgettes and quarter and seed the pepper.
**3** Arrange the vegetables on a large grill rack and brush generously with the olive oil, then grill for 15 to 20 minutes until tender and beginning to char. Turn the vegetables over halfway through and brush the other side of the vegetables with oil.
**4** While the vegetables are grilling, put the stock in a pan with the bulgar wheat, vinegar and salt and pepper to taste. Cover and simmer for 10 minutes until the grains of bulgar are tender, but still with a little bite.
**5** Drain the bulgar wheat into a bowl and keep warm. Reserve the juices and return them to the pan. You should be left with a relatively small amount of liquid compared to how much you started with.
**6** Add the butter and basil to the pan, then stir over a medium heat to make a buttery sauce.
**7** Spoon the bulgar on to plates, chop and top with the vegetables and drizzle with the sauce.

# THAI VEGETABLES WITH SATAY SAUCE AND LEMON GRASS

Time to make: 10 minutes
Time to cook: 15 minutes

Serves 2

**125 g (4 oz) trimmed broccoli**
**1 large carrot**
**125 g (4 oz) baby sweetcorn**
**1 courgette**
**salt and freshly ground black pepper**

*Satay Sauce*

**1 onion**
**2 teaspoons sunflower oil**
**1 garlic clove**
**1 cm (½ in) piece fresh root ginger**
**¼ stalk fresh lemon grass**
**60 g (2 oz) crunchy peanut butter**
**1 tablespoon soy sauce**
**½ tablespoon soft brown sugar**

You've probably guessed by now that I'm a fan of spicy foreign food, be it Chinese, Indian, Mexican or Thai. This recipe is inspired by Thai satay sauce, usually served with skewers of meat or prawns in Thai restaurants. The sauce is made with peanut butter, and peanuts are an excellent source of protein for vegetarians. I've tossed the sauce into lightly steamed vegetables and served them with boiled rice.

**1** Bring a large pan of water to the boil over a high heat; make sure the pan is the correct size for a steamer to fit over. Divide the broccoli into florets, peel and cut the carrots into chunky fingers, halve the sweetcorn if they are large and thickly slice the courgette.
**2** Place the broccoli, carrots and sweetcorn in a steamer, then place the steamer over the pan of boiling water. Season with salt and pepper, then cover and steam for 10 minutes. Add the courgette and steam for 5 minutes more until the vegetables are just tender.
**3** While the vegetables are steaming, make the satay sauce. Finely chop the onion. Heat the oil in a non-stick saucepan over a medium heat, then add the onion and fry for about 6 minutes until softened.
**4** Finely chop the garlic, ginger and lemon grass, then add them to the pan and fry for about one minute more. Stir in the peanut butter, soy sauce, sugar and 315 ml (10 fl oz) water and simmer, stirring to make a smooth sauce.
**5** Pile the vegetables on to a serving dish, pour over the sauce and serve.

# GRILLED GOATS' CHEESE WITH CRANBERRY DRESSING

Time to make: 15 minutes
Time to cook: 5 minutes

Serves 2

**2 goats' cheeses, see introduction**

**1 apple or pear**

**1 large firm but ripe avocado**

**3 spring onions**

**¼ head curly endive or lollo biondo**

**1 small head chicory**

**few radicchio leaves**

*Lime and Cranberry Dressing*

**1 lime**

**2 tablespoons sunflower oil**

**½ teaspoon clear honey**

**2 tablespoons cranberry sauce**

**salt and freshly ground black pepper**

I find grilled goats' cheese totally irresistible. As well as serving it in this salad, I often halve, grill and serve it on a walnut-oil dressed salad as a starter, on pizzas or grilled and served on top of fresh pasta tossed in tomato sauce. (If you scale down the proportions this makes a fabulous starter, too.) The goats' cheese you select, however, is very important as it needs to be covered in an edible soft rind, like that on a brie or camembert, to hold the cheese's shape as it melts. Serve with hot unbuttered toast.

**1** First make the dressing. Grate the lime rind, preferably with a zester, and squeeze the juice from the lime into a bowl or jar with a screw-top lid, then add the remaining dressing ingredients and whisk with a fork or shake together.
**2** Preheat the grill to high and line the grill pan with foil. Thinly slice the top from each goats' cheese with a sharp knife. Arrange the cheese, rind side down, on the foil.
**3** Core and slice the apple or pear. Peel, stone and slice the avocado. Chop the spring onions. Tear the endive or lollo biondo into pieces and separate the chicory and radicchio into individual leaves. Arrange on large serving plates.
**4** Grill the cheese for 3 to 5 minutes, keeping a close eye on it because if it is very ripe it will cook quickly.
**5** Carefully lift the cheese on to the salad, spoon over a little of the dressing and serve the rest separately to spoon over at the table. Serve immediately with hot toast.

**Cook's Tip**
Somerset and Welsh full-fat goats' cheeses are ideal. But if you are not a fan of goats' cheese, I've also tried this with the baby versions of soft blue brie or Cambozola with great success, too.

*Grilled Goats' Cheese with Cranberry Dressing*

# BROCCOLI WITH PENNE AND BLUE CHEESE

Time to make: 10 minutes
Time to cook: 20 to 25 minutes

Serves 2

**125 g (4 oz) dried penne**

**1 leek**

**125 g (4 oz) broccoli**

*Blue Cheese Sauce*

**30 g (1 oz) butter**

**30 g (1 oz) plain flour**

**315 ml (10 fl oz) milk**

**1 teaspoon ready-made English mustard**

**90 g (3 oz) blue cheese, such as Blue Cheshire, Leicester or Stilton**

**1 slice bread, about 30 g (1 oz)**

**salt and freshly ground black pepper**

Sometimes if my husband and I have both eaten lunch at work, all we fancy when we get home in the evening is something light. This fits the bill perfectly, as well as for a Saturday lunchtime snack. I like to serve it with grilled tomatoes, which I quickly cook under the grill as it preheats.

**1** Bring a large pan of salted water to the boil over a high heat; make sure your steamer will fit over this pan. Add the penne and cook according to the packet instructions until just tender, which should be about 15 minutes.
**2** Thoroughly rinse and slice the leek and cut the broccoli into florets. Put the broccoli and leek into the steamer over the pan of pasta and steam for 10 to 15 minutes until tender.
**3** Meanwhile, preheat the grill to high.
**4** While the pasta and vegetables are cooking, make the sauce. Put the butter, flour, milk and mustard in a non-stick saucepan over a high heat and cook, stirring constantly, until boiled, thickened and smooth.
**5** Crumble or grate the cheese, then stir two-thirds into the sauce and season well.
**6** Drain and add the pasta and vegetables, stirring so all are well covered with the sauce.
**7** Pile into a flameproof serving dish, then dice the bread and scatter on top with the remaining cheese. Grill for just a few minutes until golden.

# LEEK AND POTATO SOUP WITH CHEDDAR AND MUSTARD

Time to make: 10 to 15 minutes
Time to cook: 20 minutes

Serves 2

**30 g (1 oz) butter**
**250 g (8 oz) potatoes**
**250 g (8 oz) carrots**
**250 g (8 oz) leeks**
**500 ml (15 fl oz) vegetable stock**
**1 tablespoon ready-made English mustard**
**generous pinch ground mace or grated nutmeg**
**60 g (2 oz) mature Cheddar cheese**
**155 ml (5 fl oz) milk**
**salt and freshly ground black pepper**

I love soup, but rarely serve it as a starter. Even in small quantitites I find it spoils my appetite for the courses to come. Instead, I much prefer to serve it as a light supper or snack with some very fresh crusty bread. This soup is ideal – savoury, filling and tasty.

**1** Melt the butter in a medium saucepan over a medium heat. Peel and dice the potatoes. Add them to the butter and cook, stirring occasionally, while preparing the other vegetables.
**2** Peel and slice the carrots and thoroughly rinse and thinly slice the leeks. Add the carrots and leeks to the pan and fry for about 5 minutes until beginning to soften.
**3** Stir in the stock, mustard, mace or nutmeg and plenty of salt and pepper, then bring to the boil. Lower the heat, cover and simmer for 15 minutes until the vegetables are just tender.
**4** While the soup is simmering, grate the cheese.
**5** Pour the milk into a food processor or blender, then add 2 ladles of the soup and process until smooth. Pour back into the soup and return to the boil.
**6** Scatter in most of the grated cheese, then ladle the soup into bowls and top with the remaining cheese. Serve at once.

# THAI NOODLE SOUP WITH GINGER AND LIME

Time to make: 15 minutes
Time to cook: 10 minutes

Serves 2

**60 g (2 oz) vermicelli**
**900 g (1½ pints) vegetable stock, boiling**
**1 tablespoon sunflower oil**
**2 garlic cloves**
**1 small fresh red chilli**
**1 teaspoon grated fresh root ginger**
**90 g (3 oz) chestnut mushrooms**
**60 g (2 oz) baby sweetcorn**
**1 lime**
**40 g (1½ oz) creamed coconut**
**2 spring onions**
**15 g (½ oz) fresh coriander**
**3 tablespoons dark soy sauce**
**90 g (3 oz) fresh bean sprouts**

Flavoured with fresh ginger, coconut and lime, this is more substantial than traditional Thai soups, but the broth still has the spicy aromatic flavour so distinctive in Thai food. Shredded lime leaves are a classic Thai ingredient, but I can't buy any locally, so I substitute lime rind and juice. I think you'll agree that the results are just as delicious.

**1** Put the vermicelli into a heatproof bowl, pour over the hot stock and leave to soak while preparing the remaining ingredients.
**2** Heat the oil in a large saucepan over a medium heat. Crush in the garlic and seed and thinly slice the chilli. Add to the pan with the ginger. Thickly slice the mushrooms and slice the corn on an angle and add to the pan.
**3** Fry the vegetables, stirring occasionally, for about 6 minutes until beginning to turn golden.
**4** Meanwhile, remove the rind from the lime, preferably using a zester to get long shreds, then squeeze the juice. Grate the creamed coconut, chop the spring onions and finely chop the coriander.
**5** Drain the vermicelli, reserving the stock. Pour the stock into the soup and divide the vermicelli between 2 large soup bowls.
**6** Add the remaining ingredients, except the chopped coriander, to the pan and stir until well blended and the soup is bubbling.
**7** Stir in the coriander, then ladle the hot vegetables and broth on top of the noodles. Serve at once.

# ROOTS IN CIDER WITH CHEESE AND DUMPLINGS

Time to make: 5 minutes
Time to cook: about 30 minutes

Serves 2

**450 ml (15 oz) dry cider**

**1 vegetable stock cube**

**1 very small sweet potato**

**3 small parsnips**

**2 leeks**

**2 carrots**

**220 g (7 oz) canned sweetcorn, drained**

**90 g (3 oz) full-fat soft cheese with garlic and herbs**

**salt and freshly ground black pepper**

*Dumplings*

**90 g (3 oz) self-raising flour**

**⅛ teaspoon baking powder**

**30 g (1 oz) vegetable suet**

This is quite a hearty dish, perfectly suited for chilly autumn evenings when leeks and root vegetables are at their best. In milder weather, or for a less filling main meal, I sometimes omit the dumplings and serve the vegetables with boiled rice instead.

**1** Preheat the oven to 220C, 425F, Gas 7.
**2** Pour the cider and 150 ml (5 fl oz) water into a flameproof casserole. Crumble in the stock cube and season, then cover and bring to the boil over a high heat.
**3** While the cider and water are heating, peel and cut the sweet potato into chunky pieces. Peel the parsnips, cut away the woody cores, if necessary, and then cut into chunks. Add the sweet potato and parsnips to the pan, return to the boil and boil for 5 minutes.
**4** Trim and thoroughly wash the leeks, then cut them into thick slices. Peel the carrots and then slice them and add them to the pan with the leeks. Return to the boil, then cover, turn down the heat and simmer for 10 to 15 minutes until the vegetables are just tender.
**5** While the vegetables are cooking, make the dumplings. Sift the flour, baking powder and salt and pepper into a bowl. Stir in the suet and 4 tablespoons water and mix to make a fairly stiff dough. Cut the mixture into 6 equal pieces.
**6** Stir the corn into the vegetables. Cut the cheese into pieces and stir it into the vegetables until it melts and forms a cream sauce.
**7** Arrange the dumplings on top, then put the casserole in the oven for 10 minutes until the dumplings are firm on the outside but still soft inside. Spoon the vegetables and dumplings into bowls and serve immediately.

**Cook's Tip**
The dumplings in this recipe are baked in the oven so they are slightly crusty with a moist centre. If you prefer soft-textured dumplings, make them while the sweet potato and parsnip are boiling and cook them with the vegetables for the last 10 minutes in step 4, so they steam. Remove the dumplings and stir in the sweetcorn and cheese, then return the dumplings to the casserole.

# INDEX